ANTHROPOLOGICAL PAPERS
MUSEUM OF ANTHROPOLOGY, UNIVERSITY OF MICHIGAN
NO. 16

IROQUOIS CULTURE HISTORY IN THE NIAGARA FRONTIER AREA OF NEW YORK STATE

by
MARIAN E. WHITE

ANN ARBOR
THE UNIVERSITY OF MICHIGAN, 1961

ISBN (print): 978-1-949098-29-7
ISBN (ebook): 978-1-951519-51-3

Browse all of our books at
sites.lsa.umich.edu/archaeology-books.

Order our books from the University of Michigan
Press at www.press.umich.edu.

For permissions, questions, or manuscript queries,
contact Museum publications by email at umma-pubs@umich.edu or visit the Museum website at
lsa.umich.edu/ummaa.

PREFACE

Iroquois studies have long held a high place among the interests of professional and amateur students of North American Indian cultures. In the past, such studies have frequently served as testing grounds for previously untried methods of analysis and interpretations (Morgan, 1851; Hunt, 1940; Snyderman, 1948; MacNeish, 1952). In recent years, the major efforts in Iroquois research have been directed toward an understanding of the origin and development of Iroquois culture. Although the nature of the origin of Iroquois culture and the processes involved in this cultural change are still in doubt, much progress has been made (Griffin, 1944; MacNeish, 1952), and further efforts are warranted by the importance of the problem.

The investigation of the problem of the Iroquois origin and development will require the use of archaeological techniques; the results of such studies will have broader application. We may look for clarification of such problems as the development and movements of horticultural villages, the diffusion of culture traits, and the migrations of Indian groups in the Northeast. These findings will also provide the temporal perspective for Iroquois acculturation studies. The Iroquois have been regarded as outstanding among Northeastern groups in their cultural complexity, to such an extent that they have sometimes been classified as a separate subculture type. If this classification proves valid when tested by means of archaeological evidence, an explanation for this degree of cultural difference must be sought.

Because of the nature of Iroquois archaeological deposits and the history of field research, Iroquois archaeology poses some peculiar problems in techniques of analysis. The chronological sequence of Iroquois villages can rarely be established from superposition. Therefore, the investigation of problems of chronological order requires the use of some ranking technique which is based on typological evidence and which allows inferences about relative age. The typological data on which these comparisons are based are often far from satisfactory in quantity and documentation. The destruction of Iroquois sites in New York State precludes the possibility of acquiring many new data. Those data which are available for study are, for the most part, found in small and scattered private collections.

These limitations have led to the opinion, on my part, that further immediate research should have two aims. One focus should be on the establishment or verification of local sequences. It is only by holding geographical variations in typology at a minimum through the concentrated study of material from a restricted area that temporal differences can be ascertained. The second focus should be on the use of more refined techniques of analysis to validate the typological differences from which relative chronology can be inferred. A study of Iroquois sites in the Niagara Frontier Region held promise for achieving both of these objectives.

The results of this study served as a dissertation in partial fulfillment of the requirement for the degree of Doctor of Philosophy in the Department of Anthropology of the University of Michigan. With minor changes and omissions they are reproduced here. I am indebted to the following members of my doctoral committee for guidance, suggestions, and criticisms: Professor James B. Griffin, Chairman, Professors Richard K. Beardsley, Volney H. Jones, Howard H. Peckham, and Albert C. Spaulding.

To the chairman of my committee thanks are due for encouraging my interest in Iroquois cultural development and for many valuable discussions of the problems involved. Spaulding has provided the guidance and fostered the conviction that additional methods of handling archaeological data were needed. I am grateful to him for advice and consultation on the statistical and methodological procedure.

William A. Ritchie, New York State Archeologist, has given most generously of his time and experience for suggestions on many details of the problem. The New York State Science Service, through a Graduate Student Honorarium, supplied funds for field work and study in the summer of 1954.

Without the full co-operation of amateur students of Iroquois archaeology this study would have been impossible. I am especially indebted to Richard McCarthy and to Laverne Pechuman, whose information and collections form a major part of this work. Many others have allowed use of their collections, aided in field work, or given permission for excavation on their property. To all of them go my sincere thanks. Finally, several institutions have kindly permitted use of their collections and manuscript materials. Details of these acknowledgments will be found in the text.

Grateful acknowledgment is made to the Committee on Publications of the University of Buffalo for financial assistance to the publication fund of the Museum of Anthropology.

The editorial work and preparation of the manuscript for the printer has been done by Mrs. Clara D. Johnston of the University of Michigan Publications Office.

CONTENTS

ILLUSTRATIONS

TABLES

I

INTRODUCTION

The Niagara Frontier Region occupies a position in the northwestern corner of New York State. A chronological framework for the archaeological cultures of the larger area has been outlined for some time and is continually being verified and refined by additional field work and reinterpretations (Ritchie, 1944). Archaeological materials from the Niagara Frontier Region itself have undergone relatively little study and co-ordination with the archaeological cultures of the state as a whole. Data from the Niagara Frontier have not been considered in detail in syntheses of the culture history of the Lower Ontario and Southwestern New York areas (Ritchie, 1951; MacNeish, 1952; Emerson, n.d.; Guthe, 1958).

The term "Niagara Frontier Region" has been the designation for the region around the Niagara River and adjoining areas of Lake Erie and Lake Ontario since the days of French expansion westward. More recently the term has been synonymous with Buffalo and vicinity (Zenkert, 1934: 24). The Niagara Frontier, as here understood, includes an area approximately 55 miles in extent from north to south and 45 miles from west to east. It is bounded on the west by Lake Erie and the Niagara River, on the north by Lake Ontario, on the east by, but not including, the Genesee River and its branches, and on the south by, but not including, the Cattaraugus Creek drainage. It includes Niagara County, the major part of Erie County, and the western parts of Orleans, Genesee, and Wyoming Counties, as shown in Figure 1.

The problem of this study was the establishment of the chronological sequence of certain Indian sites which had been occupied by pottery-making groups in the Niagara Frontier Region. Although the occupation of this area by these groups was intensive, over thirty sites being reported, collections from only seven sites were suitable for analysis. A secondary problem was the selection and application of methods which would permit a reliable comparison and ranking of these seven sites in an order which would allow an interpretation of their relative age. Certain statistical techniques seemed to offer the best solution because the size and nature of the samples required quantitative analysis with special attention to conclusions stated in terms of probability.

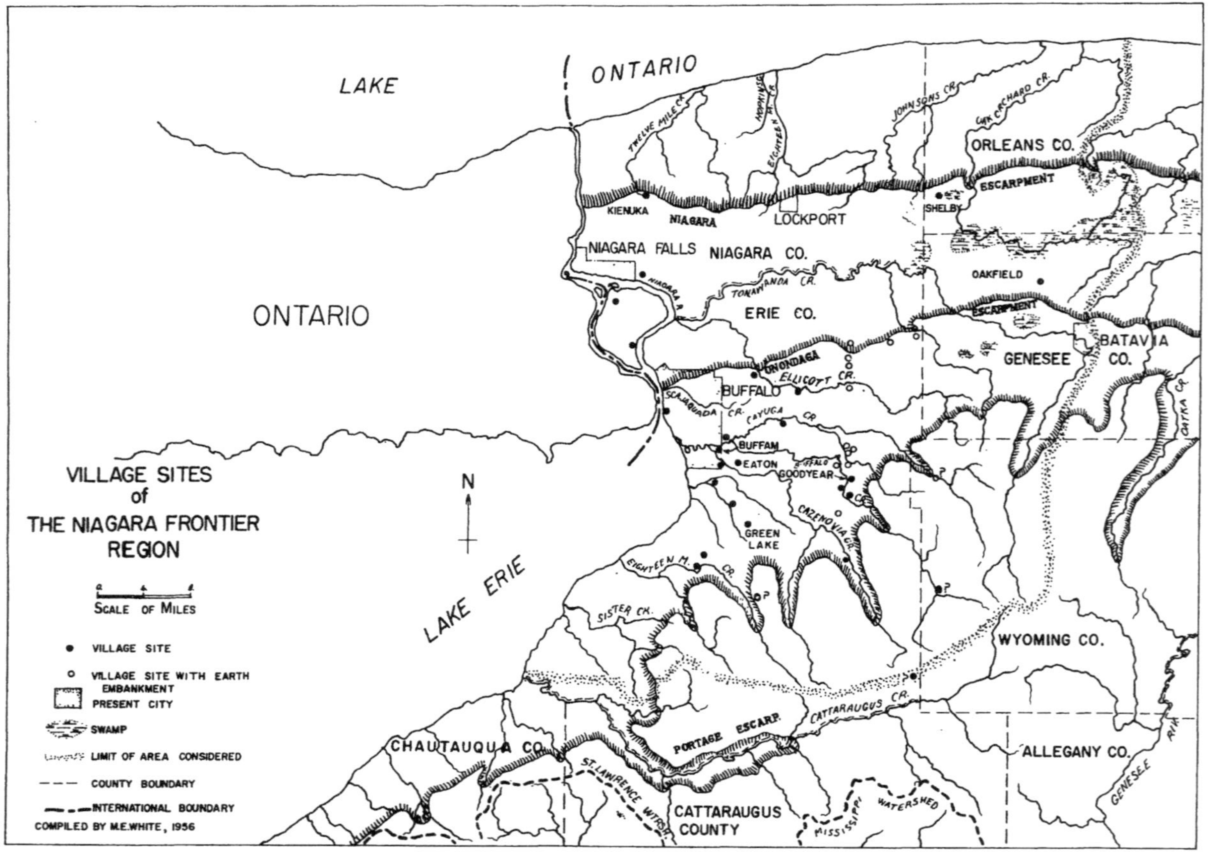

Fig. 1. Village Sites of the Niagara Frontier Region.

II

HISTORY AND PRESENT STATUS OF LOCAL RESEARCH

The history of archaeological field research in the Niagara Frontier is a hodgepodge of activities by institutions and by individuals. No institution has shown a sustained interest in the archaeology of the area, although several have done research here at diverse times. Private collectors have done most of the field work and later turned their collections over to several local institutions. The records of their field work were inadequate by current standards, and both manuscript and published accounts are generally lacking. The history of their activities has been pieced together from occasional references in the literature, museum records, and local hearsay.

The early interest in local Indians was closely associated with the growth of the Buffalo Society of Natural Sciences, which was organized in 1861 and which encouraged and occasionally sponsored archaeological field work. The names of three individuals are associated with this early activity: A. L. Benedict, Frederick M. Houghton, and Dilworth M. Silver. Benedict's collecting activities began at least as early as 1878, and his intense interest in local archaeology led him to visit those sites closest to Buffalo to make extensive surface collections. He was meticulous in recording his finds and in caring for his collections. His catalogs and field books are still available. At his death his collections were given to the Buffalo Historical Society and, in 1954, were placed on permanent loan to the Niagara County Historical Society in Lockport, New York. Inadequate care of these collections in the past led to the loss of considerable material of scientific value. When I studied these collections in 1954 there was material or information from over fifty sites in Buffalo and vicinity. Since nearly all of these sites have now been destroyed, these data were invaluable as clues to what kind of sites were once present in the area. Benedict's collections were the only ones in which pre-Iroquoian pottery (Ritchie and MacNeish, 1949) occurred. He made it a practice to save all cultural material which he found on a site, but left no written reports and was unconcerned about the cultural relationships of the data which he accumulated.

Houghton, who began his archaeological work about 1900, carried on excavations in the Niagara Frontier, the Genesee area, and the Ontario Peninsula. He is best known for his interpretations of historic Seneca material in which he became interested as a result of attempts to establish the ethnic identity of the Indian occupants of the Niagara Frontier (Houghton, 1922). The Buffalo Museum of Science which sponsored the major part of his field work was the original repository for his collections. At a later time, the material which he had excavated became part of the collections of the Buffalo Historical Society. Over the years, the bulk of his material has disappeared, and the main source of information on his work comes from published reports and a few unpublished notes which were procured by the Buffalo Museum of Science after his death. His publications include a survey of sites in the area, miscellaneous notes on his excavations, and his interpretations of the archaeology of the area (Houghton, *see* Bibliography). His researches were scholarly efforts to gain an understanding of the archaeology of Western New York.

The work of Silver is largely unknown to me. From hearsay, he apparently collected widely from sites in the area. A few artifacts which he gathered are still in the collections of the Buffalo Historical Society. He wrote one essay on the identity of the Wenro (Silver, 1923).

Somewhat later than these three, Mark Reed, of Buffalo, collected for many years from sites in the area, including most of those discussed here. His collections were purchased at his death by the Buffalo Museum of Science.

Arthur C. Parker (1922) considered the archaeology of the Niagara Frontier in his *Archeological History of New York State,* and personally carried on excavations on the Silverheels and Burning Springs Sites in the Cattaraugus Creek valley. His field work has been reviewed by Guthe (1958). In 1929, William A. Ritchie, then assistant to Parker, excavated part of the Green Lake Site at Orchard Park for the Rochester Museum of Arts and Sciences.

In recent years several individuals have been very active in collecting material from the area. Most of them have been fully aware of the importance of having an adequate documented sample from a site and so have limited their activities to a few sites. I have used their materials extensively and have profited a great deal from discussing the archaeology of the area with them. Outstanding among these are Richard E. McCarthy and Laverne L. Pechuman, both of Lockport. There are numerous others whose material was generously made available to me.

Because of the sporadic and unorganized nature of the archaeological research in the Niagara Frontier, certain limitations existed which could not be overcome by methods of handling the data. For example, the selection of sites for excavation had resulted from chance rather than from a sense of problem. Many of the collections were small, either as a result of limited excavation or loss since time of compilation. Provenience, except for the identification by site, was generally missing. Only two sites had records on depth and horizontal placement of artifacts. Most of the sites were not dug according to any plan which aimed at controlled excavation to provide a balanced sample from various features of the site. No site reports were published. No interpretations had been attempted for the area as a whole since the work of Houghton (1922).

In 1947-49, Richard MacNeish (1952) considered some of the pottery from the Niagara Frontier Region in his study and classification of Iroquois pottery. MacNeish examined the pottery from the Buffam Street and Goodyear Sites in order to make comparisons with other so-called Neutral and Erie sites in Western New York and Ontario. He used the direct historical approach in which he identified sites of the historic period with tribes and extended the sequence of tribal sites back in time by a comparison of the frequency of pottery types found at prehistoric sites.

As the major conclusion of his study, MacNeish proposed the *In Situ* theory of Iroquois culture history, which holds that several Iroquois tribes developed from variants of an Owasco base. One of these developments, according to MacNeish, took place in the Ontario Peninsula and led to a proto-Neutral-Erie-Huron group. This last group subsequently separated, and the Neutral-Erie groups entered Western New York where they subdivided into the Neutral and Erie (MacNeish, 1952: 11).

Since the advancement of the *In Situ* theory, Iroquois research has had as one of its major aims the testing of this hypothesis. One direction which this investigation might take would be the clarification of local chronological sequences by means of detailed analyses of the cultural materials from sites which MacNeish had studied as well as those from additional Iroquois and pre-Iroquois sites. The establishment of the temporal order of pottery sites in the Niagara Frontier, the problem of this study, could be expected to clarify the relationships of a number of local Iroquois sites and perhaps suggest relationships to pre-Iroquois pottery sites. Moreover, a temporal sequence in this area could serve as a means of correlating Iroquois developments in interior New York with those of Ontario and Southwestern New York. Thus the problem of the establishment of the chronological order of pottery sites in the Niagara Frontier was selected for study because it was appropriate in the light of the findings of past research and the plans for future research.

III

METHODOLOGY

Assumptions

Several basic assumptions underlie the comparative study of cultural materials for the purpose of establishing the temporal relationships among a group of archaeological sites:

1. There are demonstrable differences between the artifacts from sites in a limited area.
2. These differences result from both temporal and spatial factors.
3. In an area where distances are short and there are no geographical barriers, spatial factors are of secondary importance, so that culture can be considered uniform throughout a small and geographically homogeneous area at any single point in time.

Two of these assumptions emphasize the limited size and the geographical homogeneity required if the assumptions are to be valid. The size of the Niagara Frontier Region has been described (p. 1). A subsequent section will present the evidence that the Niagara Frontier is a single homogeneous geographical area.

On the other hand, there are no geographical barriers which delimit the area. The Niagara Frontier Region was selected for working convenience. The selection of a smaller area would have resulted in insufficient materials for comparative study; the selection of a larger contiguous area would have resulted in duplicate study of artifacts which have recently received attention. Guthe (1958) has considered materials from sites to the south, and Emerson (n.d.) those to the west. The eastern limits were drawn at the Genesee drainage to exclude a large amount of material which is scattered throughout this area — the home of the historic Seneca.

Procedure

A logical procedure in the study of the relationship of a group of sites is as follows:

1. Selection of several classes of artifacts on the basis of relative abundance, complexity, and precision of artifact attributes.
2. Comparison of the relative frequency of selected attributes or attribute combinations to provide an index of likeness for all possible pairs of sites.
3. Experimental ordering of sites to determine whether or not a systematic relationship exists with respect to the indices of likeness for all possible pairs of sites.

4. Explanation of a systematic relationship by application of some principle or principles of culture change.

Under the assumptions that have been made it would follow from this procedure that the best explanation of the differences in the site-to-site data is that these result from differences in time. Finally, a ranking of these differences will allow inferences regarding the chronological sequence of the sites.

The above procedure was the one followed in studying the temporal relationships among pottery sites in the Niagara Frontier. The following sections will describe how the procedure was applied to the data. The first step of the procedure will be described separately; the second and third steps will be discussed in a single section.

Selection of Artifact Classes and Recording of Data

Three classes of artifacts were selected for study. These were pottery, pipes, and projectile points. The experience of other archaeologists in the Northeast has shown that the first two of these are useful in indicating site-to-site differences. Projectile points met the requisites of abundance in numbers and precision of attributes, but their usefulness for comparative purposes had not been tested, and it seemed that such a test would be valuable as a guide to future research. In addition to these classes of artifacts, certain attributes of settlement pattern, burial practices, and European trade goods were taken into consideration. These were: comparative size of habitation areas, location with respect to streams, soil, topography, presence of cemeteries and ossuaries, presence of grave goods, and presence of European trade goods.

The collection of the data on the selected classes of artifacts, as well as those of the site features listed above, proceeded simultaneously with the final selection of sites and collections which would be included. The data were assembled from site collections already in existence, test excavations on two of the sites, examination of all possible sites, and a search of the literature on sites of the area. All known local collections containing these three classes of artifacts were inspected to determine their suitability for detailed analysis. There were approximately fifty collections from twenty-eight sites which contained pottery and, in most cases, projectile points. Most of these were unsuitable for analysis, largely because of insufficient numbers in the three classes of artifacts. The conditions which a collection or collections from a single site had to satisfy to be selected were these: the location of the site, collector, conditions of collection, and subsequent history of the collection must be known. The collection or collections from one site must contain approximately one hundred rim sherds of pottery. If these conditions were met, it seemed worthwhile to record the data and then to assess by statistical techniques the reliability of statements about the sample.

Seven sites had approximately one hundred rim sherds or more. These were: Green Lake, Goodyear, Eaton, Buffam Street, Shelby, Kienuka, and Oakfield. Of those sites omitted from study, none had a sample of fifty rim sherds of pottery. Some of these sites, however, provided some suggestions for a more complete picture of the culture history of the area and will be mentioned in this context.

The procedure followed in recording the data on pottery rim sherds, projectile points, pipes, and certain other attributes differed with the particular class. The way in which the pottery rim sherds were handled will be discussed first.

Pottery. — The data on the pottery rim sherds were recorded on hand-sorted punch cards. The unit of record for pottery was a single vessel represented by one or more rim sherds. This unit was selected in order to investigate its usefulness and accuracy in quantitative analysis compared to that of the rim sherd. Throughout this paper, the term, "vessels" will refer to "vessels represented by rim sherds," rather than to whole vessels, unless the latter is so stated.

The reasons underlying the investigation of the relationship between pottery rims and vessels represented by them require further discussion. Pottery is classified for two general purposes: (1) a description of the pottery-making habits of a group and the resultant products, to allow inferences leading to a description of the culture, and (2) a description of the pottery so that site comparisons may be made to arrange the sites in a specified order. The classifying procedure involves two major considerations: (1) the selection of criteria, such as attributes or attribute combinations, and (2) the selection of the unit to be counted. For the sake of efficiency, the procedure should take into account both purposes of pottery classification so that one unit may serve both. It seemed that the unit of vessel might serve both purposes more precisely and efficiently than any other.

Although the first purpose stated above is not the concern of this paper, nevertheless, the prerequisites for describing cultural behavior strongly influenced my choice of classification. To describe accurately the customary pottery-making behavior of a group with respect to the popularity of certain attribute combinations, it is often desirable that the unit counted be that on which the attributes are manifested (Spaulding, 1956: 130). Obviously, this is the pottery vessel. This is the unit resulting from the pottery-making behavior of the group and the unit which has use and function in the culture.

The second purpose, that of allowing site comparisons, is usually regarded as foremost in defining pottery types in the Northeast, where emphasis in recent studies has been placed on arrangement of sites in chronological order. For example, the pottery types currently in use by which the pottery from the Niagara Frontier might have been classified were established on the basis of "distinctive attribute combinations" (MacNeish, 1952: 2) observed on rim sherds. These criteria were selected by MacNeish because they showed "temporal or spatial (tribal) significance" (MacNeish, 1952: 2). They were quantified by counting their frequency on rim sherds, and these frequencies were compared between sites to establish the chronological order. Whole or restored vessels were included in the frequency by counting each as twenty rims.

These types were not useful in this study for several reasons. The attribute combinations often were not mutually exclusive categories. Thus the classification of a number of sherds required an arbitrary choice on the part of the classifier among several possible types. Even more important, from the standpoint of quantitative analysis, was the opinion that the frequencies based on a count of the rim sherds plus twenty rims for each whole vessel were suspect for comparative purposes.

If the number of rim sherds could be considered an accurate approximation of the number of vessels, then rim sherds could be used as the units for site comparisons. Whole vessels then could be counted as one. The relationship between rim sherds and vessels, however, is a chance one, based on position in the ground; no constant relationship can be shown to hold generally between the part, i.e., the sherd and the whole, i.e., the vessel. From observation each rim does not come from a separate vessel, nor does each whole vessel consist of twenty rim sherds. The number of rims recovered from each vessel shows wide variation. Therefore, if statements based on rim sherds are to be regarded as an accurate basis for comparing the popularity of certain pottery-making attributes, they must include estimates of how many vessels these rims represent. In some cases, especially in large surface collections, an inspection may make it obvious that nearly all the sherds represent different vessels. In other cases, a careful examination is necessary before stating statistically what the relationship is between rims and vessels represented by them.

Once this relationship between rim sherds and vessels has been ascertained, it is more efficient to use the frequency of vessels instead of the frequency of rim sherds in those cases where the number of rim sherds is not approximately the same as the number of vessels from which these came. This avoids the problem of how to handle the rim sherds when they are not a random sample of the vessels. It puts the data in a form to use for accurate statements about pottery-making behavior at a single site as well as for comparisons between sites to determine chronological order.

In order to ascertain the frequency of vessels represented by the rim sherds in this study, all the rim sherds from a collection from a particular site were sorted by inspection so that sherds of a single vessel were isolated. Also the several collections from a site were checked in this same fashion. In order to estimate the extent to which the sorting of rims into vessels might vary with the observer, one collection was independently sorted by a second observer. There was less than 1 per cent disagreement in the two results. As a final precaution in a few cases in which there was some doubt about whether two or more rim sherds might be from the same vessel, they were consistently treated as if they were from the same vessel.

A tabulation comparing the frequencies of rim sherds to the vessels represented by rim sherds for each site, under the hypothesis that this difference was due to sampling error, resulted in rejection of the hypothesis. The difference between the number of rim sherds and number of vessels for all sites would occur by chance less than once out of a thousand. The evidence for this statement is presented in Appendix A. Clearly, the rim sherds were not a random sample of the vessels. This confirmed the decision to use vessels represented as the comparative unit.

After the initial sorting into vessels, the data on each vessel were recorded on hand-sorted punch cards. Appendix B of this paper contains the card form and further information on these attributes. The following attributes or combination of attributes were noted:

1. Provenience — midden, surface, burial, or other
2. Number of sherds representing the vessel
3. Tempering material
4. Surface treatment
5. Lip decoration
6. Lip profile
7. Presence or absence of collar
8. Width of collar
9. Rim profile
10. Form — castellations, estimated mouth size
11. Collar decoration — technique, motif, and location
12. Neck decoration — technique, motif, and location

Hand-sorted punch cards were especially useful in this situation. Since the collections were widely scattered and pottery from a single site was usually in several collections, and furthermore, was not always cataloged, the use of the usual inspectional techniques for sorting sherds into categories was impractical. Second, the plan to investigate the usefulness of many attributes for classification would have been very difficult to carry out for this amount of data on each vessel by any other method. Finally, the efficiency of tabulating the frequencies and variations of attributes from punch cards is unequaled by other methods.

In summary, a preliminary inspection of all local collections containing pottery with known site proveniences led to the selection of collections from seven sites for detailed analyses of the selected artifact classes: pottery, pipes, and projectile points. The data on pottery were recorded for each pottery vessel by attribute on hand-sorted punch cards. The recording of data on the other two classes of artifacts, projectile points and pipes, proceeded by noting certain attributes of each artifact of the class.

Projectile Points and Pipes. — Data on projectile points were noted only for triangular forms two inches or less in length. This selection included the majority of points which could have been used as arrow points. The attributes used were length, width, and form. The form was described as a combination of the attributes of concave, straight, or convex sides with concave, straight, or convex base.

The sample of pipes from each site was very limited, and the specimens themselves were usually fragmentary. Therefore, written description, sketches, and photographs were the only feasible way of recording these.

Comparison of Attribute Frequencies and Ranking the Sites

After recording the data for the selected classes of artifacts, the second step in the procedure was begun. Although this procedure consists logically of two parts, selection of certain attributes and comparisons of those attributes, in practice these two could not be separated. In the case of pottery vessels in particular, the relative frequencies of any attribute showing variation which seemed to be the result of cultural behavior were computed for each site. If very little difference in frequency occurred between each pair of sites with respect to a particular pottery attribute, this classification was discarded. If considerable differences were noted, additional indices of likeness were computed, and some statistical technique was employed to determine if the differences were significant or would produce an orderly arrangement. Thus many classifications and orderings were tried and discarded as being of little use for this problem. This was due to the fact that the pottery samples from five of the seven sites were very similar in the frequency of many of the ceramic attributes, while those of the remaining two sites were different both in the presence and frequency of certain ceramic attributes.

Pottery. — For those ceramic attributes which gave promise of producing an orderly arrangement of the sites, one of these indices of likeness served as the basis for the site-to-site comparisons: (1) coefficient of agreement, (2) *phi*, a coefficient of association, and (3) simple comparison of proportion.

Robinson's coefficient of agreement (1951) gives a single expression for the similarity of a group of attributes, attribute combinations, or types at each pair of sites. For example, we might wish to state the similarities in the motifs and decorative techniques at 2 sites. Horizontal incised lines occur on 25 out of 82 vessels, 30 per cent, at Kienuka. At the Goodyear Site this same combination was found on 5 out of 266, for 2 per cent of the total. The disagreement between these 2 sites for this combination is 30 per cent minus 2 per cent, or 28 per cent. The disagreement is determined in this manner for each attribute combination of motif and technique which is being considered. These differences are added to obtain the total disagreement, called the coefficient of disagreement. The coefficient of disagreement is subtracted from 200, the greatest possible agreement. In the above example, in addition to the difference of 28 per cent, other attribute combinations of motif and technique show differences as follows: 10 per cent, 30 per cent, and 70 per cent. The coefficient of disagreement is 138; the coefficient of agreement is 62.

Phi is a measure of association for data appropriate to 2 x 2 tables (Edwards, 1946: 122). For example, we may wish to know whether collared vessels are more strongly associated with the Goodyear Site than they are with the Oakfield Site. A 2 x 2 table may be set up by placing the frequencies of collared vessels and of uncollared vessels respectively in the two columns and the Goodyear Site and the Oakfield Site respectively in the two rows. This will result in four cells, the upper left (*a*) containing the frequency of collared vessels at Goodyear, the upper right (*b*) containing the frequency of uncollared vessels at Goodyear, the lower left (*c*) containing the frequency of collared vessels at Oakfield, and the lower right (*d*) containing the frequency of uncollared vessels at Oakfield. *Phi* is then computed by the appropriate formula and will lie between +1 and -1. If the product of collared vessels at Goodyear and uncollared vessels at Oakfield exceeds that of collared vessels at Oakfield and uncollared vessels at Goodyear (*ad* exceeds *bc*), the association is positive. *Phi* will be greater than zero but it cannot exceed +1. Zero indicates no association. A negative *Phi* would show a negative association between collared vessels and the Goodyear Site. This would be the same as a positive association between uncollared vessels and the Goodyear Site.

For example, the association of collared vessels and the Goodyear Site is +.17. The association between uncollared vessels and the Goodyear Site is -.17; the association between uncollared vessels and the Oakfield Site is +.17. Thus .17, without regard to the sign can be used as a statement of the comparison of these two sites with respect to collared vessels or uncollared vessels.

In many cases the differences were further tested by the use of *chi square* to determine the probability that the difference might be due to sampling error rather than to real differences in the population (Fisher, 1941: 94). When significant or marked differences were observed between some sites with respect to a particular ceramic attribute, the statements of similarity for each pair of sites, expressed as coefficients of agreement, *phi*, or comparison of proportions, served as the basis for ranking the sites. The method used for ranking the coefficients of agreement and *phi* was that which was applied to archaeological data by Brainerd (1951) and Robinson (1951) for the chronological ordering of sites. This ranking technique was applied to the statements of similarity in the light of a hypothesis about the temporal order of the sites. A discussion of this hypothesis will follow in a later section.

Projectile Points.— The data on projectile points were tabulated to obtain the average length, average width, and standard deviations for the total sample from each site. Then the average length and the average width were examined for each attribute combination of form, such as straight sides with straight bases, straight sides with concave bases, and concave sides with concave bases, giving a total of nine possible combinations. These averages were considered in terms of the following hypothesis.

Since projectile points in the earlier Owasco culture had larger and especially wider triangular forms, a hypothesis was advanced that the projectile points would show a decrease in length and in width from early to late. The average lengths and widths at each site were arranged according to a hypothesis concerning the temporal order of the sites and were inspected to see whether this arrangement showed a progressive decrease in length and width.

The length and width for the attribute combinations of form at each site were plotted on a graph to see if the size of points for any attribute combination of form differed greatly from that of any other attribute combination of form at each site. Since no hypothesis concerning a systematic change from site to site in the form combinations suggested itself, further consideration of these seemed fruitless.

Of the several projectile point attributes which were studied, only two, average length and average width, were useful. To assess the reliability of comparisons based on these two attributes, the differences between the average length and the average width of projectile points were found for each pair of sites. Student's *t* test gave an estimate of the probability that this much difference between the means might occur by chance (Rider, 1939: 91-95). For example, the mean length at Oakfield differs from the mean length at Buffam by .18 inch. From the probability obtained for *t*, this difference might occur between five and ten times out of a hundred due to sampling error.

Pipes and Other Attributes. — The sample of pipes from each site was small. It seemed, therefore, that the use of frequencies for comparative purposes would result in uncertain judgments. For that reason the presence on Niagara Frontier sites of certain pipe forms which had a known chronological position in nearby areas seemed to be the most useful comparative factor. If these forms were time markers in other areas, I assumed that their presence indicated a similar relative chronological position for the site in the Niagara Frontier. In one or two cases, certain forms occurred frequently on some sites and were totally absent on others. If statistical tests indicated that this absence had a low probability of occurring by chance, their absence seemed significant.

The comparisons of pipes were useful in ranking the sites in chronological order in this way. The sites were ordered in terms of the hypothesis, and the presence of certain forms was compared for the sites in the area as well as with sites outside the area. These comparisons served to indicate similarities or differences between certain sites which were useful for chronological inferences.

The attributes of settlement pattern and burial practices were treated in much the same way as the pipes. The presence of certain features such as earth embankments or hillside middens, was the basis of the comparisons between sites. The absence was not entirely reliable because of the possibility of destruction by cultivation.

Finally, the independent ranking of the sites from the similarities and differences in various attributes of pottery, supported or refuted by comparisons in projectile points, pipes, and settlement pattern was examined as evidence bearing on the hypothesis which was advanced to explain the chronological relationship between the sites.

Hypothesis about Chronological Order of the Sites

A hypothesis based on my impressions about the chronological position of these sites was advanced prior to an intensive study of the data. It stemmed from a general familiarity with the material from the sites of this area and from those surrounding it. The Oakfield Site was presumed to be the earliest in the sequence because the pottery decorative technique of cord-wrapped stick impression linked it more closely to pre-Iroquoian cultures. Kienuka seemed next in the sequence because it lacked the cord-wrapped stick impressions, but had interrupted linear pottery decoration, a technique generally associated with early Iroquois sites (MacNeish, 1952: 19). The three sites of Shelby, Eaton, and Buffam were considered to be intermediate since they lacked European trade goods. Finally, the Goodyear and Green Lake Sites both produced a small amount of European trade goods and were, therefore, the latest in the sequence.

In the light of this evidence, twelve alternate arrangements of the seven sites seemed to be equally likely. These arrangements stated with the latest site first were as follows:

1.	Green Lake	Goodyear	Eaton	Buffam	Shelby	Kienuka	Oakfield
2.	Goodyear	Green Lake	Eaton	Buffam	Shelby	Kienuka	Oakfield
3.	Green Lake	Goodyear	Buffam	Eaton	Shelby	Kienuka	Oakfield
4.	Goodyear	Green Lake	Buffam	Eaton	Shelby	Kienuka	Oakfield
5.	Green Lake	Goodyear	Eaton	Shelby	Buffam	Kienuka	Oakfield
6.	Goodyear	Green Lake	Eaton	Shelby	Buffam	Kienuka	Oakfield
7.	Green Lake	Goodyear	Buffam	Shelby	Eaton	Kienuka	Oakfield
8.	Goodyear	Green Lake	Buffam	Shelby	Eaton	Kienuka	Oakfield
9.	Green Lake	Goodyear	Shelby	Eaton	Buffam	Kienuka	Oakfield
10.	Goodyear	Green Lake	Shelby	Eaton	Buffam	Kienuka	Oakfield
11.	Green Lake	Goodyear	Shelby	Buffam	Eaton	Kienuka	Oakfield
12.	Goodyear	Green Lake	Shelby	Buffam	Eaton	Kienuka	Oakfield

Throughout this paper the data will be presented according to the order of the first alternative. This order was not assumed to be more likely than any other arrangement listed but it seemed that the best arrangement could be selected only by ranking the sites independently by attributes. If one arrangement could be shown consistently to be the best one when each attribute was considered independently, it could be accepted as the best arrangement of the sites. The best arrangement could then be regarded as the best chronological arrangement under the assumption that the differences between these sites were due to differences in time rather than in space.

IV

GEOGRAPHY

The geography of the Niagara Frontier may be related to the chronological sequence of archaeological sites in the area in two respects. First, it is necessary to consider the assumption that the Niagara Frontier is a single homogeneous geographical area, without major geographical barriers. It is under this assumption that cultural differences resulting from spatial factors have been considered a constant. Second, the distribution of sites within an area may bear some relationship to geographical differences within this area. If this is the case, an investigation of this relationship may give some clues to temporal differences among the sites. The geography of the Niagara Frontier will be described first. This will provide evidence for examining the assumption that the Niagara Frontier is a single geographical area. Finally, the distribution of sites with respect to geographical differences will be indicated.

The Niagara Frontier Region has been included in two physiographic provinces, the Central Lowland and the Appalachian Plateau (Fenneman, 1938: 279, 449). The boundary between the two provinces is the Portage Escarpment, although it is not always clear which escarpment should be selected (Fenneman, 1938: 279, 449). The Appalachian Plateau, which includes the southern third of the Niagara area, was here heavily glaciated and has been classified as a separate section of the province, the Glaciated Allegheny Plateau. The rock formations underlying the plateau have a pronounced dip toward the south. As a consequence of this, the northern edges of several formations are outcrops which form three separate escarpments stretching in an east-west direction. These escarpments, the Niagara, Onondaga, and Portage, constitute the major physiographic features within the Region.

The southernmost of the three, the Portage Escarpment, is the northern limit of the Glaciated Allegheny Plateau. Here are sandstones and shales. The altitude of the Glaciated Plateau which lies within the Niagara area is between 1200 and 2000 feet. It has been classified as highland area (Cline, 1955: 6) with gentle to steep hillsides and numerous narrow valleys.

The land north and west of the Portage Escarpment, about two-thirds of the Niagara Frontier, has been classified as part of the Great Lake Section of the Central Lowland Province. This section as a whole contains at least 10,000 lakes, many swamps, creeks, and rivers. Portions of two of the Great Lakes, one major river, numerous creeks, several small lakes, and swamps are found in the Niagara Frontier.

Beginning at the north of the Great Lake Section of the Niagara

Frontier, Lake Ontario has an elevation of 246 feet above sea level. From this level the terrain rises by a series of steps, marked by the escarpments, to heights of about 2000 feet in the south where the Allegheny Plateau is encountered. On the north, the first level – the Ontario Plain, part of the Ontario-Green Bay Lowland of the Great Lake Section – parallels the present shore line of Lake Ontario. The Ontario Plain extends inland for approximately 7 miles where it is abruptly terminated by the Niagara Escarpment which rises 1 to 200 feet above the plain.

Above the Niagara Escarpment is the Huron Plain, which generally varies between 6 to 700 feet above sea level. Its extent is shown in Figure 1. The Onondaga Escarpment marks the southern extent of this plain. The escarpment is tilted in such a way that while its western end is only slightly above the Huron Plain, the eastern end where it leaves the Niagara Frontier is 80 to 100 feet above the level of this same plain.

The Onondaga Escarpment begins a third level, the Erie Plain. The Erie Plain, from 6 to 900 feet in elevation, spreads out from Lake Erie, which has an elevation of 573 feet, and follows both the north and south shores of the lake, as well as extending eastward across the area. The southern edge of the Erie Plain ends at the Portage Escarpment which also marks the northern extent of the Allegheny Plateau.

The classification of the Niagara Frontier area in two separate provinces tends to emphasize differences between north and south which, in fact, occur very gradually. Thus there is a change of approximately 1,750 feet in elevation from north to south and a change from lowland to highland; but this change takes place through increasingly elevated plains and, finally, foothills. Other differences occur in climate, soil, and vegetation. While they may be important in terms of site distribution within the area, they are not pronounced enough to present geographical barriers to the diffusion of cultural traits.

The absence of geographical barriers is clearly evident from an examination of the drainage system of the Niagara Frontier. Many of the streams have their headwaters on the Allegheny Plateau whence they flow northward across a major part of the area. There are twenty-six named creeks and many more unnamed. Sixteen of the named creeks flow in a generally west direction and empty into Lake Erie or the Niagara River. The major examples of this group are Tonawanda Creek, Buffalo Creek with its branches of Cayuga and Cazenovia, and Eighteenmile Creek (Erie County).

The rest of the named creeks, eleven in number, flow north or northeast into Lake Ontario. Most important of these are Eighteenmile (Niagara County, sometimes known as Red Creek), Johnson's, and Oak Orchard Creeks. In general, the streams of the area form an insequent drainage pattern. The streams southeast of Buffalo, especially Eighteenmile Creek and Buffalo Creek with its branches, were major rivers in postglacial times and carried a large volume of water into old Lake Erie. As the elevation increases southeast of Buffalo and especially close to the Portage Escarpment, these streams have cut broad valleys, 20 to 60 feet below the surrounding land area.

The absence of geographical barriers and the presence of a common drainage system for the Niagara Fontier support the assumption that the Niagara Frontier is a single homogeneous geographical area. With this evidence in mind, it is useful to examine the distribution of the village sites which produce pottery. If differences in distribution can be noted, two explanations seem most likely. Certain geographical features which are not shared by the whole area may be functionally related to the culture of these groups. Second, certain particular historical features, such as the successive, orderly movement of village sites from an earlier center or point of entrance into the area may account for a nonrandom distribution. Neither explanation excludes the other.

The distribution of pottery-producing sites in the Niagara Frontier is shown in Figure 1. In addition to the seven sites considered in the hypothesis, thirty-two others are included. The sources for the location of these were the surveys of Houghton (1909), Beauchamp (1900), Parker (1922), and Squier (1851), as well as unpublished notes of Houghton and Benedict (Buffalo Museum of Science). No sites judged to be historic Seneca after 1655 were included because the distribution of sites after that period was probably effected by European acculturation. Sites which produced only pre-Iroquoian pottery were omitted.

Thirty-five of the thirty-nine sites occur in the Great Lake Section of the Niagara Frontier; four are in the Allegheny Plateau Section. This is clearly a nonrandom distribution. Furthermore, the existence of none of the four south of the Portage Escarpment is certain (Houghton, 1909: 317, Sardinia; 335, Site 84; Parker, 1922: 716, Sites 6 and 7). On the other hand, the sites north of the Portage Escarpment are all known to be village sites either because of considerable cultural debris, including Iroquois pottery, or because of the presence of earth embankments. Questionable sites in the Great Lake Section were omitted.

None of the thirty-five sites occurs north of the Niagara Escarpment on the Ontario Plain. Twenty-eight sites are on the Erie Plain and seven on the Huron Plain. There can be no doubt that the Erie and Huron Plains were the sections of the Niagara Frontier in which village sites were located while the Allegheny Plateau and the Ontario Plain were without village sites.

Geographical differences between the four sections may be examined as possible explanations for the differences in site distribution. Presumably these geographical differences would be factors in the environment which are closely related to the culture of the area during the time of the pottery-producing villages. Since these sites produced Iroquois pottery, Iroquois culture may be used as an example of the culture of the area. Iroquois groups had a subsistence based on slash and burn agriculture in which corn, beans, and squash were the principal crops. Hunting and fishing were of secondary importance. Therefore, climate and soils were factors in the environment which were very closely related to the culture.

Changes in climate do occur within the area. Temperatures and length of growing season are most favorable close to Lake Erie and Lake Ontario. Temperatures are colder, and the growing season is shorter as the distance from the lakes increases. Both the ameliorating effect of the large bodies of water in the North and West and increases in elevation away from the lakes are responsible for the differences in temperature. Daily temperature readings are 4 to 8 degrees colder in Wyoming County than in Niagara County during the winter season. Of more direct bearing is the length of growing season. The length of the average growing season in Buffalo is 177 days (Zenkert, 1934: 39). The length of the growing season in Wyoming County ranges between 135 and 150 days (Cline, 1955: 7).

The effects of these climatic differences are most clearly seen in the flora of the area. There is a reversal of the zonation of the flora so that more southern vegetation forms occur in the northern Lowlands while northern forms are found in the southern Glaciated Allegheny Plateau (Zenkert, 1934: 23). The flora of the area is best classified as being part of the Alleghenian Area of the Transition Zone in which both boreal and austral elements occur. On the Glaciated Allegheny Plateau, however, flora of the Canadian Zone of the Boreal Region predominate. In parts of the Erie-Ontario lowlands the vegetation is typical of the Carolinian Area of the Upper Austral Zone.

While these differences in the flora *per se* may or may not have been important to the aboriginal populations, they illustrate important contrasts in the climate. These climatic differences were especially crucial in this environmental situation since the length of the growing season is close to the minimum of 120 days required for "reliable" corn growing (Kroeber, 1939: 212). In general, the climate and growing season of the Ontario, Huron, and Erie Plains were more favorable for aboriginal agricultural populations than those of the Glaciated Allegheny Plateau.

At least three conditions of soil need to be taken into account for their effect on slash and burn agriculture, fertility, drainage, and topography. Relative fertility can be expressed in terms of productivity for modern agriculture as exemplified by general farm crops. The soils of the Niagara Frontier show the result of glacial mixture and postglacial stream action. In general those of the Central Lowland are most productive and have the most favorable topography. Most of the Allegheny Plateau is cultivable under certain conditions and for certain specified crops, but soil drainage and erosion are major problems (Cline, 1955: 6).

North of the Niagara Escarpment, on the Ontario Plain, the soils are mainly glacial till or glacial till overlain with lacustrine deposits and stratified sands. Alluvial soils are unimportant since they come from very recently deposited sediments. The productivity of these soils for general farm crops is moderate, and lime is required for maintaining productivity. Drainage is a major problem (Cline, 1955: Soil Association Map; Pearson and others, 1947). The topography is level.

On the whole, the types of soils found on the Huron Plain are the same as those on the Erie Plain, but there is a difference in the relative amounts of particular types. For example, a greater part of the Huron Plain is dominated by soils on glacial lake or marine sediments in the west and glacial till in the east. The glacial till is generally confined to low, broad ridges. Alluvial deposits are scarce and limited to narrow valleys. The Erie Plain is also dominated by soils on glacial till with a higher proportion of silty clay loams, especially in the west. Alluvial soils occur in wide stream valleys. The soils of both Plains are predominantly grey-brown podzols of good productivity. The alluvial soils which mark a larger area on the Erie Plain than on the Huron have high productivity.

Soil drainage is poor on much of the Huron Plain. Several large swamps occur in Genesee and Orleans counties. Soil drainage is satisfactory on most of the Erie Plain. On the whole, the topography of both sections is level. The southern edge of the Erie Plain has a gently rolling topography, but here the valleys are wide and level (Cline, 1955: Soil Association Map; Taylor and others, 1929).

On the Allegheny Plateau the soil types and associations differ considerably from those of the Lowlands. Most of the soils are on glacial till with alluvial soils unimportant. Only one soil association is moderately productive for general farm crops. The soils are rocky and acid and require heavy limeing. Drainage is unsatisfactory and extensive erosion takes place. The terrain is generally hilly (Cline, 1955: Soil Association Map).

The fertile, well-drained, and level land of the Erie Plain was probably most suitable for the cultivation requirements of the native inhabitants. The soil of the Huron Plain was somewhat less favorable with respect to the proportion of fertile (especially alluvial) soil and drainage conditions. On the Ontario Plain, fertility and drainage were less suitable than on the Erie and Huron Plains. Much of the terrain is swampy. The soils of the Allegheny Plateau were infertile, rocky, poorly drained, and uneven. These soil conditions, combined with the less favorable climate and growing season, made this section of the Niagara Frontier much less suitable for an agricultural people.

Another explanation for the confinement of sites to the Huron and Erie Plains would be a historic one, based on the problem of origins and successive movements of villages and groups in the area. This can be dealt with more fruitfully in subsequent pages after a consideration of the ethnohistory of the area and after the chronological sequence has been established.

An examination of the geography of the Niagara Frontier has shown no physiographic features which might have formed geographical barriers to the diffusion of culture, thus causing cultural differences to vary with spatial differences. This is support for the assumption that cultural differences resulting from spatial factors may be considered a constant. We have noted geographical differences within the Niagara

Frontier which coincide with differences in the distribution of pottery-producing sites. No sites of this kind occur on the Allegheny Plateau which is marked by colder temperatures, shorter growing season, infertile, rocky, poorly drained soil, and uneven topography. No sites occur on the Ontario Plain where soil fertility and drainage are less suitable. The pottery-producing sites occur on the Erie and Huron Plains where the soil is fertile, especially in alluvial and well-drained valleys. Geographical differences would seem to be one explanation for the distribution of sites within the Niagara Frontier.

V

ETHNOHISTORY

The Historic Period

A study of the ethnic identity of the pottery-producing groups of the Niagara Frontier and the history of their activities in the area might conceivably provide important information for use with the archaeological data to establish a chronological framework for the area. In nearby areas it has been possible to document certain sites according to tribe and date. If this could be done for some sites in the Niagara Frontier, the results would greatly strengthen the validity of the chronological framework by providing a known point in time for a part of the sequence. Furthermore, the identification of a site with a known group would help unravel the problem of village and group movements in the area. The importance of this information to the culture history of the area justifies a somewhat lengthy discussion of the ethnohistory.

The ethnohistory of the Niagara Frontier may be said to begin in 1615 when Champlain named several ethnic groups which may have been in the area. But the selection of 1615 as the beginning of the historic period would imply a congruity between the documentary evidence and the dating of archaeological sites that is unsubstantiated. A more useful marker for the historic period is the presence of European trade goods which can be readily detected among the archaeological data. It is well known that European trade goods were present in many parts of the eastern United States before there were documents describing these parts. Some estimates of the time when European trade goods might have first reached the Niagara Frontier are important for fixing the approximate beginning of the historic period and for dating sites which can be assigned to the historic period in the absence of documentary evidence. The following sections will consider first the evidence for dating sites of the early historic period. This will be followed by a review of the documentary and cartographic evidence as it pertains to three ethnic groups, the Neutral, Wenro, and Erie.

The most precise way of fixing absolute dates for sites of the early historic period in the absence of documentation would be by accurate identification and dating of the changes of style which European trade goods underwent in the local area. If carried to a sufficient degree of refinement, this would allow the dating of sites from the earliest contact with Europeans which resulted in the local Indians obtaining European goods. Since such a system has not as yet been worked out for the Niagara Frontier, this leaves two alternatives: (1) a consideration from history of when trade goods might have become available, under the assumption that the Indians generally would adopt them as soon as possible, thus giving a possible beginning date for the historic period, and (2) a consideration of when they became available on sites in adjoining areas where the chronology has been worked out, as verification of the possible time for the beginning of the historic period.

European trade goods, which might have reached the Niagara Frontier marking the beginning of the historic period and for some time thereafter, would have been obtained from other Indians acting as middlemen, since European traders had not penetrated far into the interior. Estimates of the sources and quantities of trade goods available become clearer after an examination of the history of discovery and exploration of the Northeast and the European policies of trading with the Indians.

Although French official claims to the New World were based on the discoveries of Verrazano in 1534, it is clear that some knowledge of the North American continent existed much earlier. French Bretons and Normans were fishing regularly on the Grand Banks in the early sixteenth century. Contact was made with the natives, and in 1501 Corte-Real sent sixty Indians from the Newfoundland area back to Europe (Brebner, 1955: 93-95). Some exploration took place. In 1508 Thomas Aubert of Dieppe sailed up the St. Lawrence for 80 leagues and returned to Europe with an Indian (Thwaites, *Jesuit Relations*, Vol. III: 38; hereinafter cited as *JR*, 3: 38). Basque sailors carried on whaling activities from Tadoussac and the Saguenay River (Brebner, 1955: 120). The area around the Gulf of St. Lawrence gradually became a trading, as well as a fishing center (Brebner, 1955: 121).

Beginning in 1534, there were more permanent contacts between Europeans and Indians as settlements were attempted and explorations of the interior began in earnest. In 1604, Sieur De Monts led a group, including Champlain and Pontgravé, which settled first in Acadia and then moved to Port Royal. This marked the beginning of permanent settlement in two parts of New France. Certainly, trading with the Indians was one of the major purposes for establishing settlements. An examination of the policy of trading will bear this out.

About 1581, European traders began to take the initiative in seeking furs from the Indians rather than allowing the Indians to make the trek to the Gulf of St. Lawrence (Brebner, 1955: 121). At first trading was free from government restriction. A group of merchants from St. Malo, France, took the lead and sent vessels up the St. Lawrence to intercept the furs on the way to the Gulf of St. Lawrence (Brebner, 1955: 121).

In 1588, the French government granted a monopoly of the fur trading to members of the Cartier family. This was soon revoked as a result of strong protests by French merchants. When De Monts, in 1608, founded a settlement at Quebec, a group of Rouen merchants financed the enterprise. The Company of Associates, organized by Champlain from merchants of other trading centers, took charge in 1611. Under French policy the main interest of all these companies was financial profit since, on the whole, they represented private enterprise. Their profit lay in the exchange of European trade goods for furs. There was little interest in settlement or missionizing, except for that of the French Recollects and Jesuits.

In brief, from about 1500-1525, trading with the Indians was certainly incidental to fishing but undoubtedly some exchange took place. This marks the possible beginning for trade material in the Niagara Frontier. Trading for furs became progressively more important until, by 1580, it became the major purpose for some voyages. Shortly thereafter, special companies were organized for trading and the trading centers moved slowly toward the interior, following the St. Lawrence.

Probably most of the trade material which reached the Niagara Frontier during this time passed through the hands of Indians in Canada. Beginning at least as early as 1609, Hurons and Algonquins came annually to trade at Quebec. In the *Relation of 1639*, Father Le Jeune (*JR*, 16: 229) said concerning the Hurons, "It is about forty years since these peoples for the first time resolved to seek some safe route by which to come themselves, and trade themselves with the French, of whom they had some knowledge, —particularly through the reports of some of their number, who, going to engage in war against their enemies, had occasionally been at the place where the French were at that time trading with the other barbarians of these countries." The Huron at that time transported large quantities of European goods westward where they exchanged them for furs and other commodities. It is known that they traded with the Neutral for corn and tobacco (Fenton, 1940: 188). Since the Huron were friendly with the Iroquois groups who were not part of the Five Nations, it seems likely that they would have exchanged European trade goods with the Indians of the Niagara Frontier.

Dutch explorations and settlements in New Netherlands may have been another source for obtaining European goods during the early historic period. It is doubtful that these were of as much importance for the inhabitants of the Niagara Frontier during the early historic period as were those of the French. The Mohawk were the middlemen in Dutch trading. Trade goods would have had to pass through the hands of several tribes which lay between the Mohawk and the Niagara Frontier. Furthermore, Dutch trading was rather limited prior to 1615. Therefore, it seems that Dutch trade material was probably unimportant in this area during the early historic period. The trade goods found on sites in the Niagara Frontier, perhaps as early as 1500 and thereafter, probably had their immediate source in Canada whence they had been obtained from Europeans and especially French, via the St. Lawrence.

It is possible to assess these remarks about the beginning date for trade goods and the subsequent increases in quantity by a comparison with nearby areas in which the dates are firmly established. The best comparison is with the Seneca area to the east. Here a sequence has been established for protohistoric and historic sites, and absolute dates have been assigned with a high order of accuracy. Wray and Schoff (1953: 53-63) have located seven successive Seneca sites, the latest of which is documented at 1687. Assuming 15 to 25 years for the occupation of each site, the earliest pair of the sequence, the Adams and Tram Sites, date between 1550 and 1575. European trade goods are very scarce. The authors feel that their source was boats off the Atlantic Coast (1953: 54). The sites of the next period, 1575-90, show a noticeable increase in trade material (Wray and Schoff, 1953: 55). These data suggest that European trade goods did not reach the Seneca area as early as might be expected from the historic records of contacts with Europeans, or that they occurred in such small quantities that they have not been found archaeologically. A conservative date for the beginning of European trade goods in the western New York area is probably 1550 with a rapid increase in quantity after 1575.

These same conclusions probably apply to the Niagara Frontier Region. Native inhabitants here might have been in a more favorable position than the Seneca to acquire trade objects from the Hurons because of proximity and friendliness, but in a less favorable position geographically to obtain goods from the Atlantic Coast. Trade goods were probably present in small quantities by 1550-75, although they might be missed in small-scale excavations. From 1575 to 1600 trade goods would probably be plentiful enough so that some would be found in surface collecting or refuse digging. The period 1550-75 will be considered the beginning of the historic period in the Niagara Frontier Region.

Documentary and Cartographic Evidence for the Early Historic Period

The ethnohistory of the Niagara Frontier begins in 1615 and may be subdivided into three periods: (1) 1615 to 1655, (2) 1655 to 1779, and (3) 1779 to the present. The first period, which will be referred to as the early historic period, begins with the travels of Samuel de Champlain and the reports of his explorations which included some information on the area. For this period there are no first-hand accounts by Europeans known to have been in the area. This period ends with the time of the accounts of the defeats of the Erie, the last tribe which may have been in the area prior to the westward expansion of the Seneca. The selection of the date of 1655 is arbitrary since the decisive battles leading to the routing of the Eries occupied several years, and it is not clear when the fighting ended.

The second period covers the time when the Niagara Frontier was frontier country for the League of the Iroquois and when the main Seneca villages were still in the Genesee country. The end of this period is 1779, when General Sullivan destroyed the Seneca villages and large numbers of Five Nations Iroquois fled into the Niagara Frontier soon to establish settlements. The third period is marked by the gradual decline in power of the League of the Iroquois, land squabbles with whites, and finally settlement on reservations, three of which are still in existence in the area. This paper will consider only the first period in detail and summarily the beginning of the second.

For the period from 1615 to 1655 it is impossible to limit discussion to the Niagara Frontier Region since the historic references are usually too indefinite to permit certain recognition of the area. Instead, it is necessary to work with the location of various ethnic groups as these are recounted in the documents or given on the maps. By a process of elimination, however, many tribes can be passed over since their location is definitely known to be outside the Niagara Frontier during the early historic period.

It is clear from the documentation of the location of numerous surrounding tribes that the Niagara Frontier lay in the midst of an area of Iroquoian-speaking peoples (Fenton, 1940: 178-79). To the east of the area, in the Genesee country, were the Seneca, the westernmost member of the League of the Iroquois. To the west, occupying most of the Ontario peninsula, were the Neutral. The other known Iroquoian-speaking tribes have been located even farther from the area, except for two, the Erie and Wenro. This paper will consider the Erie and Wenro in some detail to discover whether the references to these groups might allow their location within the Niagara Frontier. In addition, some attention will be given to the eastern boundary of the Neutral since this may impinge upon the Niagara Frontier. The Neutral will be considered first.

The Neutral

The ethnohistory of the Neutral has been given detailed attention by several authors, and their area of occupation is generally accepted as being the heart of the Ontario Peninsula (Coyne, 1895; Harris, 1896; Houghton, 1909; Jones, 1909; Fenton, 1940). Since they were a populous tribe, their villages covered an unknown extent of land east and west. Because of this and certain references which will be discussed, several authors have placed the eastern Neutral villages in the Niagara Frontier.

Samuel de Champlain (1922, III: 99) first referred to the Neutral tribe in 1615 as "la Nation neutre." He located them as follows: "at two days' journey from them [Hurons] in a southerly direction... [the Neutrals live] westward of the lake of the Onondagas." The lake of the Onondagas was Lake Ontario.

On Champlain's map of 1632, he located the Neutral Nation west of Lake Ontario. Lake Erie, however, was either omitted entirely or, as Crouse claims (1924: 34), was confused with the Niagara River. On the map there is no legend naming the stream which connects Lake Huron (Mer Douce) and Lake Ontario. The only reference that might indicate

Champlain's knowledge of Lake Erie is in Volume I (pp. 153-57), where Champlain recounts a very confused tale told him by an Indian about lakes and connecting rivers. Regardless of whether Lake Erie was indicated in the description or confused with the Niagara River on the map, the stream mentioned above which connected Lake Huron and Lake Ontario flowed directly east into Lake Ontario. Therefore, it became necessary cartographically to locate the Neutral Nation on the map with respect to the river, if this group was to be placed west of Lake Ontario. From the text, it seems that the important point which was known to Champlain was the location of the Neutral west of Lake Ontario rather than their location in relation to the river, which is unmentioned. On the basis of Champlain's map, it cannot be assumed that he meant to indicate that the Neutral villages were located east of the Niagara River in the Niagara Frontier.

The next information about the Neutral country comes from Father Daillon, the Recollect, who visited several of their villages in 1626. There is no statement that the Father saw the Niagara River. In one passage he referred to a river which may be the Niagara. He explained that the Neutral were eager to go to trade with the French but did not know the route. Yroquet, an Algonkin, who was trapping beaver in Neutral territory at that time, refused to disclose the location of the mouth of the "River of the Iroquois" which would take them there (Sagard-Theodat, 1866: 798-809). Severance, who claimed that the "River of the Iroquois" usually referred to the St. Lawrence, thought that in this case it might have included the Niagara River, of which the St. Lawrence could be considered a continuation (Severance, 1917: 16). Houghton (1909: 272) accepted this as reference to the Niagara, and Crouse (1924: 39) also considered it likely.

It is difficult to understand the Neutrals' lack of knowledge of the mouth of the Niagara if any of their villages were located at that time in the vicinity of the river. On the other hand, this reason given by the Neutrals to Daillon might have been intended to placate the Hurons present, who were trying to prevent direct trade between the Neutral and the French. The Father may have been correct, however, for the Neutral were notoriously poor canoesmen (Galinée, 1917: 172; Fenton, 1940: 188; Hunt, 1940: 51, 96). It is possible that the Neutrals' knowledge of the Lake Ontario-St. Lawrence route to Quebec was limited by their practice of land transportation. Furthermore, since their only enemy was the Fire People (Mascoutins?) to the west, their knowledge of geography to the east might have been limited (Champlain, 1922, III: 99-100). Again there is no conclusive evidence locating the Neutral villages east of the Niagara River in 1626.

A later reference placed the Neutral group clearly on the east side of the Niagara River, as well as on the west. Father Lalemant (*JR*, 21: 187-91), reporting in 1641 on the journey of Fathers Brébeuf and Chaumonot to the Neutral in 1640, stated that there were about forty villages and that the nearest was 40 leagues south of the Huron country.

"On this side of that River [Niagara], —and not beyond it, as a certain Chart indicates, —are the greater part of the villages of the Neutral Nation. There are three or four beyond, ranging from East to West, towards the Nation of the Cat, . . . and at the end of that Lake, it enters into the territory of the Neutral Nation, and takes the name of Onguiaahra." He also referred (*JR*, 21: 209) to Onguiaahra as the last village on the East, "but a day's journey" from the Seneca.

The above passage implies two things: (1) that the Neutral territory included both sides of the Niagara River, and (2) that the village Onguiaahra was near the river Onguiaahra or Niagara. Jones has placed it near Youngstown, New York (Fenton, 1940: 187). Youngstown is approximately 75 miles from the Power House Site, a Seneca village of 1630-50 (Wray and Schoff, 1953: 57). Clark has estimated that a day's journey for an Indian was 25 to 30 miles on foot (Murray, 1931: 21). This would place these two locations three or four days' journey apart and does not agree with the statement of Lalemant. One must conclude either that (*a*) Onguiaahra was not near the Niagara River, or (*b*) the Senecas had villages or more likely controlled territory west of the Power House Site, or (*c*) Onguiaahra was more than a day's journey from the Seneca. The second alternative seems most likely since at this time the Senecas had begun to expand westward for new beaver grounds, a topic which will be discussed more fully under the treatment of the Wenro. There is no evidence for choosing among these alternatives, however, and the location of Onguiaahra must remain questionable.

The part of the statement that the Neutral villages extended from east to west toward the Erie becomes clear if Lalemant had in mind the geography of the Niagara Frontier portrayed on Champlain's map of 1632. Here the Niagara River flowed directly east. In this situation villages beyond, but parallel to, the river would extend from east to west toward the Erie.

Crouse (1924: 27) discussed the unnamed map referred to by Lalemant as placing the Neutral group incorrectly east of the Niagara River. He claimed that there must have been a missing manuscript map of unknown authorship to which Lalemant was referring. It seems that Champlain's map of 1632, published in 1633, will fit the reference equally well. I have also presented a plausible explanation of why the Neutral Nation was drawn east of the Niagara on this map. My conclusion from the above remarks is that while we have evidence in 1640 for the location of three or four villages east of the Niagara River, this does not warrant the assumption that they were there at an earlier period, or that the Neutral, therefore, occupied any extensive part of the Niagara Frontier.

More recent authorities have reached various conclusions from the above evidence about the extent of the Neutral in the Niagara Frontier. Confusion on two points accounts for much of the disagreement: (1) the identity of the Wenro, who are considered by some authorities as part of the Neutral and by others as a separate group, so that some include Wenro territory in their definition of Neutral territory while others do not, and (2) the definition of Neutral territory compared to the location of Neutral villages. The location of the villages is of prime interest to the archaeologist since he possesses no evidence for the assignment of territory that was unoccupied by settlements.

Fenton (1940: 186) stated, "Their [Neutral] territory . . . extended from well east of the Niagara indefinitely west of Detroit River and Lake St. Clair, for they had villages just east of that river; it embraced all of southern Ontario north of Lake Erie to a line drawn from Oakville below Toronto to Goderich on Lake Huron . . . Down to 1639 their eastern member, the Wenro, inhabited a row of 4 villages stretching west toward the Erie."

In Fenton's statement above it is not clear to me whether he was including the Wenro when he placed the territory of the Neutral "well east of the Niagara," or whether he considered that the Wenro lay beyond this in some direction. On Fenton's accompanying map indicating the Iroquois position from 1600 to 1650, he located the Neutral west of the Niagara and the Wenro east, until 1639 (Fenton, 1940: 178-79).

Fenton's information on the location of the Neutral villages was based on the work of Jones (1909). Jones' definition (1909: 291) of the Neutral area is similar to that of Fenton, except that he omitted the statement about its extent well east of the Niagara. In a second definition (1909: 422), he stated that the Neutral country lay within the Province of Ontario except for three or four outposts east of the Niagara. Jones (1909: 423) claimed that the three or four villages, including Onguiaahra, were those of the Ouenrohronons, or Wenro, whom he regarded as a "Neutral tribe." Fenton has accepted this.

Father Lalemant in his report written in 1641, but referring to the Neutral in the autumn of 1640, did not indicate that the three or four villages in question were Wenro villages. Nor do I think we can assume that Father Lalemant was talking about Wenro villages and failed to mention it. For in the same *Relation* (*JR*, 21: 231-33), Lalemant mentioned some people "of a certain strange nation who had dwelt beyond [*au dela de* which also means "on the other side of"] the Erie or Cat Nation, called Awenrehronon," who had taken refuge in a Neutral village to escape their enemies. He clearly recognized a difference between Neutral and Wenro. The Wenro group had been driven out of their traditional home, and in August or September, 1638, some were arriving in Huron country. In 1639, Lalemant (*JR*, 17: 25-27) described their arrival in an account written two years before his statement about the Neutral villages. Therefore it seems highly unlikely that he would have confused the Neutral and Wenro, especially since the Wenro villages were no longer in existence when he made the statement in 1641. Without much doubt he was referring to Neutral villages and not Wenro when he mentioned villages east of the Niagara. He added (*JR*, 21: 191-93), as further proof, "After all, I believe that those who formerly ascribed such an extent to this Nation [Neutral], and assigned to it so many tribes, understood by the term 'Neutral Nation,' all the other Nations, which are South and Southwest of our Hurons,—which indeed are very numerous, but which in the beginning having been only confusedly known, were comprised almost under one and the same name. The greater knowledge which we have gained since that time, both of the language and of the country has made us more discriminating."

Houghton (1909: 268) did not include the Wenro when he said of Neutral territory, "Eastward it extends across the Niagara River as far at least as Lockport. East of the Niagara it extended at least as far south as Tonawanda Creek, and perhaps to Eighteenmile Creek." In a later publication (1920: 34) after considerable excavation and study of archaeological materials from Ontario, Houghton made some additional pertinent statements. He noted that the Neutral were probably moving slowly from west to east since all the sites west of the Grand River in Ontario lacked European trade material while those east had trade materials in increasing abundance as the Niagara River was approached. This statement of Houghton's does not agree with Jones' locations of Neutral villages. The two were using different kinds of evidence, the former archaeological, the latter historical. Furthermore, Houghton's observations probably apply to a limited number of sites on which he worked rather than to all Neutral villages. Houghton's statement is certainly well worth keeping in mind as a hypothesis for future testing.

On the basis of four diagnostic artifact types, Houghton located three Neutral villages east of the Niagara River. All had trade goods. These were located at Kienuka, Grand Island, and East Hamburg (Houghton, 1920: 28-36). MacNeish (1952: 11) agreed on the identification of the Grand Island Site. Houghton (1909: 376-85) reported on this site, but did not describe the material in detail. Most of it has now been lost. I was unable to form any opinion from the small amount in the Buffalo Historical Society. The presence of abundant trade material and especially a Jesuit ring, would probably place the site after 1630, judging from the Seneca sequence (Wray and Schoff, 1953: 63). The situation at Kienuka will be discussed in a later section. The third site at East Hamburg is poorly known, but there is the information that it had abundant European material.

Houghton's identification of these sites as Neutral rests solely on typological evidence. I am not convinced that the limited archaeological evidence which he cites has been shown to be sufficiently limited in distribution to serve as a basis for assigning any of the above-mentioned sites to the Neutral or to any specific group. In brief, there is no satisfactory documentary evidence in Champlain's accounts or in the description of Sagard's visit to the Neutrals in 1626 to indicate that Neutral villages were located east of the Niagara prior to 1626. In 1640, there were several east of the Niagara according to Father Brébeuf's observations. The archaeological evidence for these is inconclusive. The documents provide no precise location. My own opinion from the scant facts of ethnohistory is that a few Neutral sites were east of, but in the vicinity of the Niagara River, for a very short period, beginning about 1630.

In 1647, the first of the Neutral villages, Aondirronon, was destroyed by the Seneca. Jones (1909: 440) claimed that this was one of the villages east of the Niagara. The only evidence for this is cartographic and will be discussed below. Two documentary notes may suggest that no Neutral villages were east of the Niagara in 1647. Gendron (1868: 6-8) in a letter written in 1644-45 from New France located the Neutral south of the Huron and north of Lake Erie. He described Niagara Falls and the rapids in the Niagara River. Finally, he noted certain unnamed Indians living around the Falls, implying that these were not Neutral. In the *Relation of 1647-1648,* there is a tale of a young Huron girl who was captured and taken to a Seneca village (*JR*, 33: 95-97). She escaped and traveled about three days, meanwhile crossing a river. She met four Indian men who recaptured her. Two favored returning her to the Seneca. The other two, Neutrals, claimed that since she had crossed the river she was in their country and, therefore, could continue. They gave her food and directed her to their villages, whence she was taken back to Huronia. This river may have been the Niagara. The Niagara is the only large stream which would be encountered in going west from the Seneca villages after crossing the Genesee. Admittedly the evidence is very poor. If this river was the Niagara, then the villages at this time, 1647, were west of the Niagara River. The other villages mentioned in the continuation of the Neutral-League war until 1651, have been located west of the Niagara (Jones, 1909: 328). My conclusion from the documentary evidence is that the several Neutral villages which moved east of the Niagara stayed in the vicinity of that river, for a brief period only, probably 1630-45.

An examination of the major maps from 1632 to 1700 supports the location of the Neutral west of the Niagara. I have already discussed Champlain's map of 1632. The Sanson map of 1650, "Amérique Septentrionale," located them west of the river and from this time on they are shown in approximately the same position on most of the maps (Fig. 2). This uniformity of location is undoubtedly because Sanson's maps served as the major influence in French cartography for some time to come (Karpinski, 1931: 32). The sources for the Sanson map of 1650 were the reports and explorations of the Jesuits (Crouse, 1924: 46). Therefore, one would expect the position of the Neutral to correspond with the verbal location given by the Fathers. This is hardly independent evidence on their location.

There are four maps which give additional or contradictory evidence:

DuCreux map of 1660, "Tabula Novae Franciae"
Bernou (?) map of 168? (Lake Erie)
Franquelin map of 1684, "Carte de la Louisiane"
Delisle map of 170?, "Tire des Relations des Hurons de 1639, 1640, et 1641"

Fig. 2. A Section of the Sanson Map of 1650.

Fig. 3. A Section of the DuCreux Map of 1660.

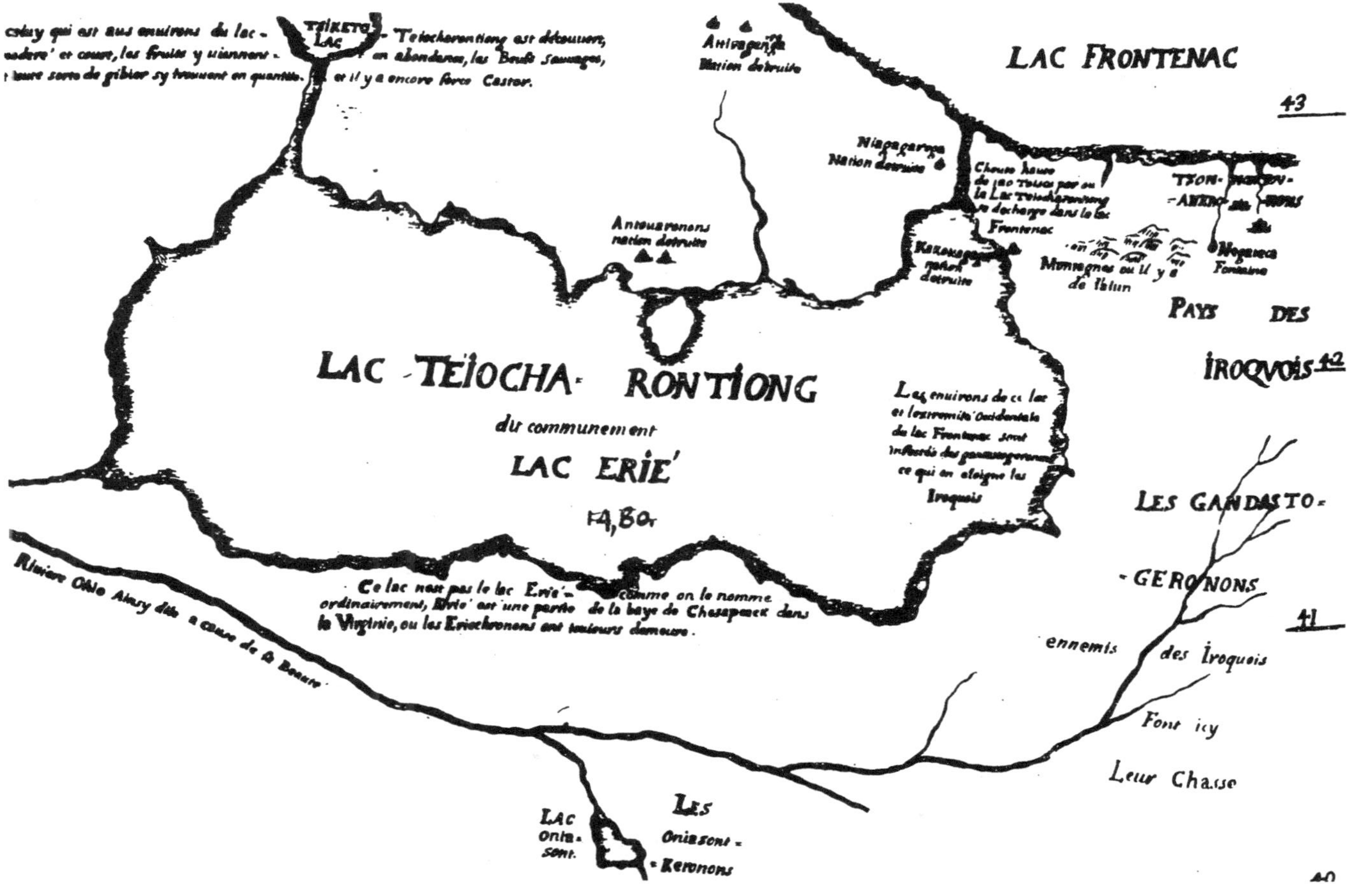

Fig. 4. A Section of the Bernou (?) Map of 168?.

Fig. 5. A Section of the Franquelin Map of 1684.

The DuCreux map used essentially Sanson's outline of Canada and the Great Lakes, but contained much additional information on Indian tribes (*JR*, 46: Frontispiece; Karpinski, 1931: 32). It is important to remember that DuCreux, also known as Creuxius, was never in Canada (Crouse, 1924: 48). His map was certainly based on the Jesuits' accounts. Jones (1909: 5-6) has criticized it for minor inaccuracies in geography and questionable locations in the Huron country.

On the DuCreux map (Fig. 3), "Gens Neutra" is shown east of Lake Ontario. Jones (1909: 423) claimed this map showed the Niagara Neutral by the word "Ongiara" west of the Niagara River. I interpret this as belonging with the word "catarracts" immediately below so that the legend reads "Ongiara catarracts." If this is the correct interpretation, the Niagara Neutral are not indicated.

East of the Niagara River and west of the Genesee, there is the large caption "Ondieronii." Above this is "p. Ondiaraius" and below is "Ondieronius pagus," near which are two village markers. There is obvious confusion as to which group of people these names refer. Jones (1909: 440) equated this with Aondionons and Ahondihronnons (*JR*, 18: 233; 33: 81; 42: 197). Only in one of these references (*JR*, 33: 81) is this group further identified. In 1647, they were part of the Neutral closest to the Hurons. At this time they were destroyed by the Seneca.

Jones accepted DeCreux' location of the Ondieronons east to the Genesee and concluded that this group of the Neutral extended across the river for a considerable distance on either side. But there is no textual information placing villages east of the river in 1647, and certainly not as far east as the Genesee, because the Seneca had been expanding westward since 1639 at least.

Although the DuCreux title implies that the map refers to 1660, this cannot be the case for the Neutral since they were already dislodged. It is a guess whether the map portrays the Neutral at a single limited time period, or whether it is cumulative in its information. For this reason, cartographic evidence can be very misleading.

My conclusion is that the DuCreux map is useless for locating a group in Western New York. MacNeish (1952: 10) disagrees on the value of this map. Because of the criticism directed at the DuCreux map by others and especially since the source and the date of the information is unknown, I do not find it necessary to modify my conclusions about the Neutral extent in the Niagara Frontier as a result of this map.

The Bernou? map of 168? is one of a series of unpublished sketch maps discussed at length by Delanglez (1938: 34-39; 1941: 115). These maps have generally been attributed to Jolliet, but Delanglez presents convincing evidence that they were the work of Abbé Claude Bernou and were probably drawn in 1680. The map of interest for the Neutral is that of Lake Erie shown in Figure 4 (Doysie, No. 111 in Clements Library, 4044B48 in Paris Archives). Before taking up the information it contains, it is well to consider the possible source of the information, if the cartographer was Bernou. Bernou had available the information of LaSalle, for whom he was the major promoter. On several occasions he is known to have used letters from LaSalle as sources of information for maps and descriptions of New World geography (Delanglez, 1941: 115). It seems likely that LaSalle's letters were also the source for new information or locations on the Lake Erie map.

On the Lake Erie map, the legend "Atiragenrega, Nation detruite," occurs west of Lake Ontario. This is probably a variation of Atiroguenek or Atirhangenrets which Jones (1909: 439) considered synonymous with Attiwandaronk or Neutral. West of the Niagara River is the legend "Niagaraga, Nation detruite." There is no indication that this "Nation" is part of the Neutral, but it probably is. Elsewhere we have noted that Ongniahra was a Neutral village. One village marker is shown on the Lake Erie map clearly west of the Niagara River in the area of the "Niagaraga Nation."

LaSalle's information has not always proved to be accurate and he certainly was not in the Neutral area until after their defeat. On the other hand LaSalle was in the Neutral area in 1669 and again in 1679 when he spent considerable time on the Niagara while the Griffon was being constructed. It is probable that the Seneca Indians with whom he had contact on both these occasions could have given him first-hand information on the Neutral.

On Franquelin's map of 1684 (*JR*, 63: Frontispiece), in addition to a notation in west-central Ontario, "Ou estoit la Nation Neutre," in eastern Ontario by the Niagara River is the notation "atiragennagora, det. [detruit]." This map is shown in Figure 5. Atiragennagora is probably another variation of Atiraguenek or Atirhangenrets which Jones (1909: 439) claimed to be the Attiwandaronk or Neutral.

The Delisle map, based on the Jesuit accounts of 1639-41, is one of a series of twenty-four unpublished sketch maps drawn by Guilliame Delisle in preparation for the 1703 map of America, which Delanglez (1943b: 274) claims was drawn in final form by the Father, Claude Delisle. These were probably prepared between 1700 and 1703 and are obviously taken from the *Jesuit Relations*, as marginal notations indicate. Photostatic copies of these maps are in the Ayer Collection of the Newberry Library, Chicago, and in the Dominion Archives in Ottawa.

It was probably the sketch map mentioned above which MacNeish (1952: 10) used for his identification of the Buffam Street Site as historic Neutral. He was uncertain of his identification. In my opinion, it is completely unwarranted, both historically and archaeologically. The location of the four villages east of the Niagara River is probably based entirely on the statements which the Fathers made and which contain no definite location. The legend on the map by these villages seems to be a paraphrase of Father Lalemant's statement (pp. 26-27). Therefore, it seems that the location of these villages was no better known to the map-maker than to us. Even if the location was accurate, the villages could not possibly be considered to be at Buffalo since they are beside the Niagara River about half way between the lakes. But I do not feel this information is reliable enough to give further consideration. In short, none of the cartographic evidence offers further information on the location of Neutral villages or the extent of their territory east of the Niagara River.

There has been a tendency among certain archaeologists to ascribe some archaeological materials in the Niagara Frontier to the Neutral. The summary of the documentary and cartographic sources has indicated that the evidence for the geographical and temporal extent of the Neutral occupation east of the Niagara River is far from conclusive. Clearly a few villages were east of the Niagara, but probably for a very brief time, such as 1630-1645. It is at present impossible to document these sites.

Further confusion arises from the original sources as the result of various names for groups or villages which may or may not have been part of the Neutral. We must even question our notion that there was a single group of Indian villages which identified themselves by a group name and which corresponded approximately in size and extent to what the French called Neutral. The term may have been applied by the French to a number of groups which did not regard themselves as members of a single unit or tribe. This possibility must be kept in mind. The situation can be clarified archaeologically by a careful comparison of archaeological materials in the Ontario Peninsula, across the area supposedly occupied by the Neutral, and further careful comparison with materials from the Niagara Frontier.

If distinctive cultural traits can be ascertained for historic sites west of the Niagara River in Neutral territory, then these same traits can be used for comparison with historic sites in the Niagara Frontier. Pottery will probably prove the most useful. If comparisons show that historic sites on both sides of the river have a very similar cultural complex, then other comparisons must still be made. Sites of the same period would be expected to be similar in their culture as a result of geographical proximity, even though they may have been occupied by groups with different tribal affiliation. For this reason, it will be necessary to find traits that will link some but not all of the historic sites in the Niagara Frontier with those of Ontario, since it is probable that sites of additional groups were present in the Niagara Frontier in early historic times. Therefore, the traits selected must distinguish between these groups.

The ultimate test would be the connection of certain historic sites in the Niagara Frontier with Neutral sites in Canada by tracing the movements of villages from Ontario across the Niagara Frontier, in late prehistoric or early historic times. Since the name, "Neutral," is the designation for historic villages and by extension for their immediate predecessors in that area, its application to sites should be limited to those which connect directly with the historic Neutral in Canada. This is the only way of distinguishing Neutral sites from those of other groups which might have moved into the Niagara Frontier earlier and have had a very similar development to that of the Neutral in Ontario.

The Wenro

The Wenro group has been included by some authorities as part of the Neutral group (Hewitt, in Hodge, 1912, Pt. 2: 932). Yet the Jesuits clearly distinguished the names, locations, and histories on several occasions. In the *Relation of 1639* (*JR*, 17: 25-27), Father Lalemant stated: "The Wenrohronons formed in the past one of the associate Nations of the Neutral Nation and were located on its boundaries toward the Hiroquois." These people made a journey of "more than eighty leagues" to reach the Huron village of Ossossane. Lalemant mentioned them again in the *Relation of 1640-1641* (*JR*, 21: 231), as having formerly lived beyond the Cat Nation, or Erie. Hewitt (Hodge, 1912, Pt. 2: 933) interpreted this to indicate that the Wenro lived on the upper waters of the Allegheny or possibly on the west branch of the Susquehanna and were one of the tribes called the Black Minquaas or Mingo. Hewitt (Hodge, 1912, Pt. 2: 933) translated the name Awenrohronon as "the people or tribe of the place of floating scum" and suggested from that their location near Oil Springs, Cuba, New York. Although the archaeology of the area around Cuba is very slightly known, no village sites have been reported from that vicinity.

Other evidence for the location of the Wenro stems from the possible identification of the village Ouarorono. In 1626, Father Daillon (Sagard-Théodat, 1866: 807) met ten men from the last village, Ouarorono, one day's journey from the Iroquois. These men came to trade in the Neutral village of Ounontisaston where Daillon was staying. If Ouarorono is considered Neutral and the statement of its location accepted, then there were Neutral villages east of the Niagara in 1626. I have already discussed other evidence which led to my conclusion that there were no Neutral villages east of the Niagara in 1626. In order to be consistent with this conclusion which I feel is based on stronger evidence, I do not interpret Daillon's statement about Ouarorono to mean that it was a Neutral village. Daillon's text perhaps implies that it was Neutral. At the time of Daillon's visit there is no record indicating that Wenro (or Erie) had been identified by name. It seems likely that Daillon used Neutral to include groups which the Jesuits distinguished by another name by 1639. If he meant to indicate that Ouarorono was a Neutral village, this does not necessarily mean that Neutral here refers to the same group which the Jesuits meant by the term Neutral.

The identification of Ouarorono as a Wenro village is more consistent with my arguments and interpretations of other information. Houghton (1920: 36) reached the same conclusion and considered Ouarorono a possible variation of Oenrorononons. It is reasonable that this slight difference (*ua* cf. *en*) might have resulted from language difficulties (Daillon had an Algonquin interpreter), miscopying of his manuscript, or from a variety of possible explanations. The location of the Neutral and Wenro with respect to the Seneca and to each other is clearer if Ouarorono is interpreted as a Wenro village.

Houghton (1920: 40), on the basis of the Wenro's location toward the Iroquois from the Neutral and the distance of their journey to the Huron, places them near Oakfield or Elma, New York. He identified the sites at Buffam Street, Eaton, Oakfield, and Shelby with this group. Archaeological evidence does not support this identification, for all these sites are prehistoric. The Wenro had trade goods before their departure to Huronia in 1638, for Father Bressani (*JR*, 39: 141) mentioned that they had traded with "English, Dutch, and other heretical Europeans." The Wenro do not appear on any map of the Niagara Frontier Region. The documentary evidence is not sufficiently clear to locate them. They probably lived in the Niagara Frontier, between the Neutral and Seneca, but no more definite location can be given.

A consideration of their brief history gives some insight into the events which were taking place in the area prior to 1655. In August or September, 1638, the Wenro abandoned their territory and took refuge among the Neutral and Huron. The main body presumably went to the Huron, but some were in the Neutral village of Khioetoa or St. Michel in 1640 when Brebeuf and Chaumonot passed through. The Fathers said (*JR*,21: 231-33), "Some years ago, . . . there took refuge in this village a certain strange Nation, who had dwelt beyond the Erie or Cat Nation, called Awenrehronon." Du Peron (*JR*, 15: 159) described a nation who had fled to Ossossane, Huronia, "on account of the Hiroquois, their enemies, and of the epidemic, which is still causing great mortality among them."

Lalemant (*JR*, 16: 253) identified these people as the "Weanohronons . . . a nation of the Neutral language . . . who formed one of the Nations allied with the neutral Nation." Later in the same *Relation* (*JR*, 17: 25) he gave a description of their arrival at Ossossane. "As long as this Nation of Wenrohronons was on good terms with the people of the Neutral Nation, it was sufficiently strong to withstand its Enemies [the Iroquois], to continue its existence, and maintain itself against their raids and invasions; but the people of the Neutral Nation having, through I know not what dissatisfaction, withdrawn and severed their relations with them, these have remained a prey to their Enemies; and they could not have remained much longer without being entirely exterminated, if they had not resolved to retreat and take refuge in the protection and alliance of some other Nation."

The Wenro sent ambassadors to the Huron in advance, asking permission to join their group. The Huron agreed, according to the Jesuits, because they saw that the Wenro arrival would serve "not a little for the defense and preservation of the country" (*JR*, 17: 27). Six hundred Wenro, mostly women and children, arrived by foot, many having died along the way. The Huron went out to help them with their baggage and to protect them. The time of their arrival can be fixed in late August or early September. On their arrival they were distributed among the Huron villages where many of them were cared for and baptized by the Jesuit Fathers (*JR*, 17: 29-31).

Thus the Wenro were the first of the surrounding groups to be displaced by the League of the Iroquois in their quest for new hunting territory. There seems little reason to doubt that this was the major reason for the Seneca's increased warfare. By 1640, the Iroquois had exhausted the beaver supplies in their own territory (Hunt, 1940: 69-74). Certainly beaver were becoming scarce in the years preceding this. The Wenro territory probably offered the best opportunity for the Seneca's expansion, and some hostilities had broken out before 1638. The Wenro were a small group, possibly one or two villages, judging from the six hundred survivors. These were mostly women and children, and the population had already been reduced by disease. Because of disease and fear, the Wenro moved out, and in 1638, their territory probably became Seneca frontier country.

The Erie

The Erie group was first mentioned in 1635 (*JR*, 8: 293) and was included again in a listing of tribes made in 1640 by Father Le Jeune from a map drawn by Father Ragueneau (*JR*, 18: 233-235). Lalemant (*JR*, 21: 191), in 1641, located the Neutral with reference to the "Lake of Erie, or of the Nation of the Cat" and placed the Wenro beyond the Cats. He did not, however, give the location of the Erie or Cats. The first definite information appeared in a letter written in 1644-45 by Gendron (1868: 8) and was repeated in the *Relation of 1647-1648* (*JR*, 33: 63) where Ragueneau described "a great lake nearly two hundred leagues in circumference, called Erie; . . . This Lake called Erie, was formerly inhabited on its Southern shores by certain tribes whom we call the Nation of the Cat; they have been compelled to retire far inland to escape their enemies, who are farther to the West."

The names of two villages are associated with the Erie — Riqué and Gentaienton. The first, Riqué, from which is derived the name "Riquehronnons who are the Cat Nation" has been translated "at the place of the panther" (*JR*, 45: 209; Fenton, 1940: 195). Tradition has made Riqué the capital of the Erie Nation and the village of the final defeat. Some have placed it at Erie, Pennsylvania (Hewitt, in Hodge, 1912, Pt. 2: 392; Carpenter, Pfirman, and Schoff, 1949: 6). No reason is given for this identification of the capital or its location. Shetrone (1919: 311) repeated the identification in *The Indian in Ohio* and many popular accounts have taken it up. In the *Relations*, there is no evidence connecting Riqué with the Erie village destroyed by the Seneca in the final battle with the Erie. The location of Riqué and Gentaienton will be considered further under the cartographic evidence.

From the primary documentary evidence, it is possible to conclude that, prior to 1645, the Erie were south of Lake Erie. Also prior to this date they were forced to move inland which may mean away from the shore toward the east or south. The Erie have been located over widely divergent areas by different authorities. Before reviewing these opinions, it is well to consider what might be implied by the name Erie or Cats. The Fathers indicated clearly that they consisted of "tribes" or different groups. Furthermore, the French seemed to use the term geographically to refer to all the Iroquoian-speaking people south of Lake Erie. For example, this is the only name appearing on Sanson's map of 1650, south of Lake Erie (Fig. 2). Gradually, more names appeared, and some of these may well have once been included as "Eries." Fenton identified the Honiasont as Black Minquas and believed that these were a branch of the Erie (Fenton, 1940: 196). Certainly the Erie were a populous people credited with two to three thousand warriors (*JR*, 42: 179). This may be compared with the figures for the Iroquois League of an average of two thousand warriors (Snyderman, 1948: 41).

The Erie, regardless of their socio-political organization, occupied a considerable expanse of territory. One would expect to find differences within their culture at any given time period since different parts of them would be in contact with different neighboring groups. If the term "Erie" is a geographical one, rather than an ethnic or political one, then its application to certain archaeological remains would be meaningless, unless a village can be well documented as an Erie village. I shall show from the cartographic evidence that the term "Erie" can be applied to an Iroquoian-speaking group which lived in the Niagara Frontier in early historic times. This does not imply that this group was the only one included in the term "Erie." The people referred to as Erie in various accounts may not have had all their villages in Western New York in early historic times or at any time. But there were some in Western New York to which the term "Erie" properly applies.

The following maps will be referred to in the discussion:

Sanson map of 1650, "Amérique Septentrionale" (Sanson, Atlas of 1658)
Sanson map of 1656, "Le Canada, ou Nouvelle France" (*ibid.*)
Sanson map of 1656, "Le Nouveau Mexique et la Floride" (*ibid.*)
DuCreux map of 1660, "Tabula Novae Franciae" (*JR*, 46)
Franquelin map of 1678, "Carte pour servir a l'éclairessment du Papier Terrier de la Nouvelle France" (Clements Library, Doysié, No. 13)
Franquelin map of 1678, "Carte gnlle de la France Septentrionalle" (Winsor, IV: 218)
Franquelin map of 1684, "Carte de la Louisiane" (*JR*, 63)
Bernou(?) map of 168? [Lake Erie] (Clements Library, Doysié, No. 111)
Coronelli map of 1688, "Partie Occidentale du Canada ou de la Nouvelle France" (Karpinski, 1931: 103)
Hennepin map of 1697, "Carte d'un tres grand pais nouvellement découvert dans l'Amerique septentrionale" (Winsor, IV: 253-54)
Delisle map of 1703, "Carte du Canada ou de la Nouvelle France" (Karpinski, 1931: opposite 40)
Franquelin map of 1708, "A Monseigneur le Comte de Pontchartrain, 1708" (Clements Library, Doysié, No. 84)

The Erie are first shown on Sanson's map of 1650 (Fig. 2), as "N. du Chat." This legend began at the northeast corner of Lake Erie at its junction with the Niagara River. It ended just above an unidentified stream which I will discuss below. The legend extended east so that it included the territory up to the Genesee River.

The identity of the stream which bounded the southern extent of the legend is more difficult to establish. One landmark that remains recognizable for some time on future maps is a stream flowing southeast from Lake Erie and ending in a crescent-shaped lake. This is probably Chautauqua Lake, New York. Coyne (1903: XV) has further discussion of this point. Lake Erie is here represented with too narrow an extent from east to west so this crescent lake is considerably farther west than Chautauqua Lake. The shape of the lake is distinctive. A comparison with Sanson's map of 1656 (Fig. 6), "Le Canada," shows that the latter map emphasizes the thinness of the crescent even more, and a constriction occurs in the middle of the crescent. On the Sanson 1656 map, "Le Nouveau Mexique," the constriction is drawn as a very short stream connecting two separate lakes, but maintaining the orientation of the crescent as on the 1650 and the other 1656 map. A comparison of this shape with that of Chautauqua Lake leaves little doubt that the two are very similar. Furthermore, the retention of the general shape with slight modification suggests that this shape was intentional rather than whimsical.

On all three maps a stream flows northwest from this lake to Lake Erie. This is incorrect if the lake is Chautauqua, since Chautauqua is part of the Mississippi watershed and drains southeast. A small stream, Little Inlet, does flow into Chautauqua Lake from the northwest. About one and one-half to two miles northwest of the headwaters of Little Inlet are the headwaters of Chautauqua Creek, which flows into Lake Erie. Moreover, the direction and shape of this Chautauqua Creek-Little Inlet connection corresponds quite well with that of the stream connecting Lake Chautauqua and Lake Erie on the Sanson maps of 1650 and 1656, "Le Canada," less closely with the 1656 one of "Le Nouveau Mexique," although the general direction of the latter is accurate.

Chautauqua Lake was well known as a part of the water route from Lake Erie to the Allegheny River (Beauchamp, 1892: 75; Wallace, 1953: map). There seems to be no reason to doubt its use from late prehistoric times. A knowledge of this route would explain the features on the Sanson map of 1650 southeast of Lake Erie and northwest of the Allegheny Mountains. South of the crescent-shaped lake, which I shall refer to henceforth as Chautauqua Lake, is a river. This was drawn so that it ended abruptly on the south and terminated in a lake on the north end. A comparison of this last lake on the 1650 map with the 1656 "Le Canada" shows that on the latter map it is represented as a fingered body of water. This closely resembles the shape of the headwaters of

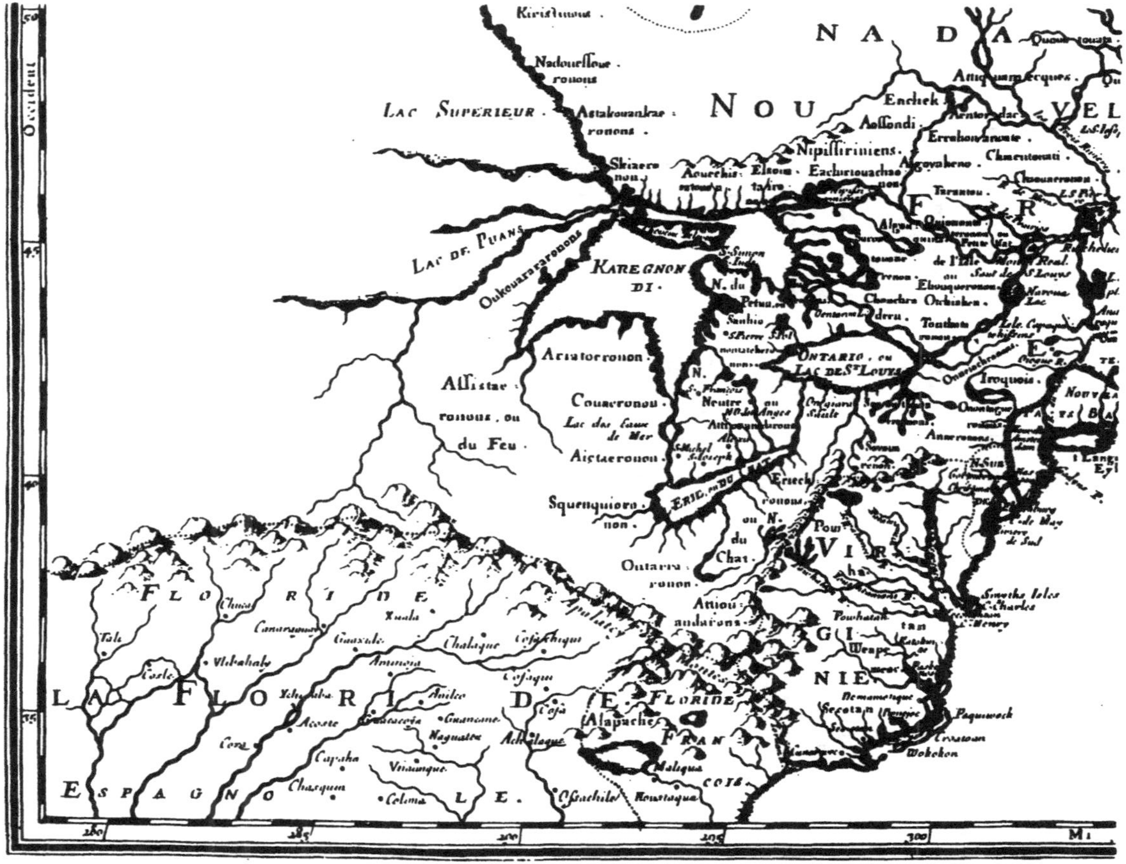

Fig. 6. A Section of the Sanson Map of 1656.

the Allegheny River in eastern Cattaraugus County, New York, and McKean County, Pennsylvania. Throughout this area the Allegheny is joined by a number of streams from the north and south and flows through a wide, swampy valley, which might well appear as a fingered, narrow lake.

It is not difficult to account for the information on this route being relayed to Europeans in Canada. There was considerable intercourse between the Hurons and the Andastes on the Susquehanna River from the first accounts in 1615 (Champlain, 1922, III: 54-58). Probably the Lake Chautauqua route was one of those used. It seems likely that the Canadians knew of this route by 1650, from the Hurons. This, then, is supporting evidence for the identification of Lake Chautauqua.

If the identification of Chautauqua Lake is convincing, then the general location of the Erie group from the Sanson map of 1650 is clear. Approximately half way between the stream flowing into Lake Erie from Chautauqua and the northeast end of Lake Erie was another stream. A reasonable guess at the identity of this would be Cattaraugus Creek, the most prominent stream in this approximate location. Cattaraugus Creek was immediately south of the end of the legend, "N. du Chat." The legend extended north to the junction of Lake Erie and the Niagara River. On the east it reached to the Genesee which here did not extend far enough south since its present branches come within a few miles of the Allegheny drainage. The western limits were the Lake Erie shore. The eastern limits seem to be governed by the size of the legend rather than by an attempt to indicate a territorial boundary. The north-south extent of the legend, however, may have been intentional since it is not limited here by the space on the map. My conclusion is that Sanson has clearly shown the Erie on the 1650 map extending from the end of Lake Erie, near the present city of Buffalo, to Cattaraugus Creek and from the Lake Erie shore to the east for an indeterminate distance.

It is well to consider the sources of Sanson's information and the period of time to which he might have been referring. As previously indicated, the general source for the map of 1650 was the Jesuit accounts. Crouse, after considerable study of the various known sources available to Sanson, concluded that it was impossible to account for his information from those sources. Both in the outline of the Great Lakes on the 1650 map and the names of the Indian groups on the 1656 map "Le Canada," there were new, unaccounted for data. Crouse (1924: 26) concluded: "The delineation of Lakes Ontario, Erie and Huron, both in their own contours and in their relations to one another conform so accurately to the work of modern surveyors that it must have been done by someone on the spot with well informed guides at his elbow. So far as we know Lake Erie, the western part of Lake Huron, and Lake Ontario (save the eastern portion traversed by Champlain) were unexplored regions when Sanson depicted them with such amazing accuracy." On the basis of this conclusion it seems that the location of the Erie can be assigned to this same unknown source and accepted with the same reliability. Sanson's reputation for honesty and accuracy are attested to by the incompleted outlines of Lake Superior and Lake Huron (Karpinski, 1931: 31).

The time at which the Erie might have been at this location is open to question. The 1650 map is the only source depicting the Erie before their defeat in 1655. However, Gendron's statement in 1647-48 (1868: 8) indicated that the Erie moved "far inland" prior to the time of his writing. If Gendron's statement is interpreted to mean away from the shores, this map either shows their former position, or they did not move far from the shores.

On the Sanson map of 1656, "Le Nouveau Mexique," the Erie were identified as "Eriechronons" (Eriechronous?) and were in approximately the same location. One change appeared in the geography of the Niagara Frontier. Two streams were added to the shore line between Cattaraugus Creek and the Niagara River. The Erie were shown between the farthest north stream and the one previously identified as Cattaraugus Creek. This placed their northern limit slightly farther south than on the 1650 map.

On the Sanson map of 1656, "Le Canada," three more streams were added in this area (Fig. 6). These details may not have been added because of increased knowledge. The incorrect identification of one of these, however, would not disturb the location by more than 10 or 15 miles, an unimportant amount in the gross terms of locations with which we are dealing. The present six streams from north to south, beginning at the northeast corner of the Lake, are: Buffalo, Smoke's, Rush, Eighteenmile, Sister's, and Cattaraugus. The legend "Eriechronons," began below the third creek which may be Rush Creek. It is certain that the legend was noticeably farther south than on the 1650 map and not far from Rush or possibly Eighteenmile Creek. On the south, the legend extended to Chautauqua Creek and Chautauqua Lake. Once again there is no way of knowing the period of time to which the map refers. None of the groups was indicated as being destroyed. The defeat of the Neutral was implied, however, by the location of the name, "Attiouandarons" in two diverse places, in the Ontario Peninsula and south of Lake Chautauqua. The Neutral's final defeat came probably in the spring of 1651. This suggests that the map represented the period following 1651. This would date after the move reported for the Erie in 1644-45 and would show their new position. If this interpretation is correct, the move made before 1644 was in a southerly direction, bringing the Erie closer to Chautauqua Lake.

It is important to note that from 1656 on for the next forty years there were no noticeable improvements in the knowledge of the geography of the western New York-Lake Erie area. This suggests that the maps of this period must be regarded with particular suspicion since there was no first hand information. Furthermore, the tribes under consideration had certainly been destroyed. DuCreux's map of 1660 (Fig. 3) depicted Lake Erie less accurately than the former ones, and the changes were obviously made from a base of the Sanson maps. Here the creek flowing into Chautauqua Lake was much longer, and this lake, if it is the same one, had lost its characteristic shape. The stream identified as the Allegheny River had disappeared. The Erie were placed west of the stream flowing into Chautauqua Lake (?) and would have been in east central Ohio. Because of the poor representation of the geography and the questionable reliability of other locations, I have little confidence in this location of the Erie.

The next major cartographer whose outlines were widely used was Franquelin. On his map of 1678, "Carte pour seruir a l'éclarrissement," an "Iroquois village" was shown at the west end of Lake Ontario. This was probably the same village referred to by Galinée (1917: 189) as Tinawatawa in 1669 when he met LaSalle there. West of the Niagara River was a village, "Kanenoke," which I assume to be a League or Seneca village, rather than Neutral or Erie, neither of which was shown.

In a second map of his of the same year and one often erroneously attributed to Jolliet, "Carte Gnlle de la France," the Seneca were shown at the east end of Lake Erie (Delanglez, 1948: 78-79). During the early years of Franquelin's drafting in Canada when he produced the above maps, he presented contemporary information on the Indians of the Niagara Frontier, and this area was then clearly inhabited by the Seneca or mixed villages of the League. There was no information on the Neutral or Erie.

At the time of the production of the famous Franquelin map of 1684, the cartographer was in Paris in the employ of LaSalle. The "Carte de la Louisiane" was drawn to show LaSalle's journeys, and the information was largely drawn from LaSalle and his lost larger map (Delanglez, 1943a: 34, 60). It seems probable that the information pertinent to the Niagara Frontier came from LaSalle. He had been in the area on several occasions between 1669 and his return to France in 1683. Delanglez discounted LaSalle's discovery of the Ohio and claimed that some of the cartographic information on the Franquelin map of 1684 was derived from Jolliet's larger map, which Franquelin drew in 1675 from Jolliet's lost original (Delanglez, 1948: 78-81). The Franquelin map of 1675 did not contain the information I am about to mention and, therefore, this information on the Franquelin 1684 map must be attributed to LaSalle or some unknown party.

On this last map a village, "Rakouagega," was located by a stream on the east shore of Lake Erie. The outline of the eastern end of Lake Erie was so poorly represented that the location of this village is doubtful. Fenton has suggested that this stream might be Cattaraugus Creek and that the name "Rakouagega" referred to Riqué, the Erie village (Fenton, 1940: 195). South of here, on a stream which is the Ohio-Allegheny, very poorly represented, was "Kentaientonga, 19v. detruits." Fenton identified this as Gentaienton, the other known Erie village. Here, however, the reference was to a group of nineteen villages.

As indicated previously, Gentaienton was noted in 1679 as a village of the Erie. In three other places there is mention of the Gentague-tehronnons as a group, without further identity (*JR*, 42: 197; (Gentagega) *JR*, 58: 75; (Kentaientonga) Margry, 1876, II: 236-37). This last reference is a letter of LaSalle's, dated 1681 or 1682 and certainly connected with the reference on the map. Thus it is not clear whether the term, "Gentaienton," referred to a village of the Erie, a subdivision of the Erie, another name for the Erie, or a separate group. Furthermore, since it cannot be shown that LaSalle was in the Ohio-Allegheny area prior to 1684, and since his information on tribes in the Ohio Valley is of questionable worth (Griffin, 1943: 26), I think we can draw no conclusions from this information.

The Bernou(?) map of Lake Erie (Fig. 4) contained some additional information on the area. The cartographer located "Kakouagoga, nation detruite," at the northeast corner of Lake Erie. This lake was named "Lac Teiocha-rontiong, dit communement Lac Erie." My translation of the legend beneath this lake is as follows: "This Lake is not Lake Erie, as people usually call it. Erie is a part of Chesapeake Bay in Virginia, where the Eries have always lived." A legend at the southeast end of the Lake translates as follows: "The land around this lake and the western end of Lake Frontenac [Ontario] are infested with Gantastogeronons [Andastes] who are different from the Iroquois." The legend, "The Andastes, enemies of the Iroquois are here for their hunting," appeared in the headwaters of the Allegheny, which are located too far north. Coronelli's Marly Globe of 1683 used the same name for Lake Erie and had a similar inscription about the Andastes with the added information "who have been destroyed for a few years at the request of the Iroquois" (my translation from Delanglez, 1938: 38). I have been unable to check the original source here, or to determine whether Kakouagoga was shown on the Marly Globe. If Delanglez is correct in dating the Bernou map of Lake Erie before 1681, then Bernou was the first cartographer known to have shown Kakouagoga. Records show that Bernou furnished maps and information for the preparation of Coronelli's Marly Globe in 1683 (Delanglez, 1941: 113). Bernou is probably the source for Coronelli's information on the Andaste as well as the location of Kakouagoga on the later Coronelli maps.

If Bernou was the source of Coronelli's information on Kakouagoga and if Bernou's information is prior to 1681, a good case can be made for the source of Bernou's information being LaSalle. LaSalle had written Bernou describing his discoveries beginning with August 7, 1679 (Delanglez, 1941: 56). A part of this first letter, covering the activities from August 7, 1679 to January 1, 1680, is missing. The missing part is known to have included the voyage of the Griffon and probably other information on the Niagara Frontier since some description of these events was later included in Bernou's *Relation des descouvertes et des voyages du Sieur de la Salle* which was based on LaSalle's earlier letters (Delanglez, 1941: 57). There is no mention of Kakouagoga in the extant portions of LaSalle's letters or in Bernou's *Relation*. But the fact of the missing part which was the one most likely to have contained the information on Kakouagoga makes arguments about the origin of Kakouagoga insolvable. On the later Coronelli maps, Kakouagoga continued to appear. On the 1688 map the "Nation du Loup" was located just below Kakouagoga, which is here slightly farther south. Swanton (1952: 48) has identified the Loup as Delaware.

The identification of Kakouagoga or the Kahkwas has been a subject of debate since the days of Schoolcraft. Houghton (1909: 302-4) has summarized the leading opinions, and there seems nothing further to add. If the Kahkwas were the Erie, we know no more than we did previously, namely, that they were located at the east end of Lake Erie. If they were not, then we have the name of a new group about which we know nothing.

The several remaining maps deal with a period nearly fifty years after the groups with which we are concerned left the area. It becomes increasingly difficult to determine whether subsequent changes are based on new information or on adaptations from earlier maps. Maps of this late date must be used with considerable caution, and I shall mention several very briefly.

On the Hennepin map of 1698, the Erie were located south of the lake formerly referred to as Lake Chautauqua. But this lake was very far west, perhaps in the vicinity of Cleveland. The representation of the lake was very poor.

The Delisle map of 1703 located the Erie south of Lake Erie, in approximately northern Pennsylvania or southwestern New York. This map was known to have been based on sketches drawn from the descriptions in the *Jesuit Relations* so represents no new information (Delanglez, 1943: 275-98).

Finally, the Franquelin map of 1708 further confused the location of the Erie. The Ouabache (Wabash) River was shown with three long branches flowing toward the northeast. The middle one was the "River Teiocarontiong ou de la Nation du Chat." This branch extended very close to Lake Erie. The territory of the Erie was south of the Lake, along the shoreline, for nearly the full east-west extent of the Lake, and well down into the Allegheny drainage. The Ontario Peninsula was labeled "Pais des Hurons." If this and the delineation of the Wabash are any indication of the accuracy of the remainder of the map, it would be well to ignore the location of the Erie on this map.

In summary, I believe that the most reliable information that can be obtained about the Erie comes from the Sanson maps. His work was most nearly contemporary with the occupation of the Erie, and he evidently had some first-hand information on the Niagara Frontier geography. Second, his maps were drawn before the era of trying to establish "first discoveries" or "territorial claims" and at a time when accuracy of description was important for future exploration.

From his maps, the Erie first lived from near Buffalo to Cattaraugus Creek, probably toward the lake shore. This may have been prior to 1644-45, although the map showing them in this location is dated 1650. Later, perhaps after 1651, and before their defeat in 1655, they had moved south, inhabiting the area from Rush or Eighteenmile Creeks to Chautauqua Lake. I have little confidence in later maps which place them farther west. It seems clear that they were located in the Niagara Frontier, along the lake plain, and from the site distribution in general, north of the Portage Escarpment. When the archaeology of this area becomes better known, it will be possible to make comparisons with sites of the Allegheny drainage and the lake shore farther west to test movements into this area.

Other authorities have assigned a wider territory to the Erie than I am willing to accept from the evidence. Fenton (1940: 194-95) located them from Eighteenmile Creek, across northern Ohio, and down the Allegheny River to Pittsburgh and a short distance down the Ohio. One reason for this extent was his identification of the Honniasont as Erie (Fenton, 1940: 195-96; Hunt, 1940: 102). The identification of these groups and the territory occupied by them is beyond the scope of this paper since, clearly, they were not located in the Niagara Frontier.

Houghton (1920: 41) believed that the most easterly village of the Erie was at Ripley, New York, as Parker (1907: 525-31) had suggested, and, therefore, he did not ascribe any sites in the Niagara Frontier to them. Other identifications and accounts of the Erie stem from quite different sources from those I have considered. These have been made by historians and antiquarians from Swedish and early Pennsylvanian and Ohioan documents. None of these are concerned with the Niagara Frontier Region. The dates of these documents are later than the Sanson maps and the *Jesuit Relations,* and their perspective of geography derives from an increased knowledge of the Pennsylvania-Ohio area from the Atlantic seaboard as explorations were pushed farther and farther into the Ohio valley. These appear to deal with the Erie after their defeat when remnants of them were scattered in various places. In these accounts the Erie are variously identified with the Shawnee, Cherokee, Tuscarora, and Massawomecks. Hanna (1911: 12-18) has summarized the major opinions advanced on the identity of the Erie. None of these seem satisfactory for establishing the early historic location of the Erie and only add to the confusion. It seems, therefore, that the identification of Erie archaeological remains should start from the Niagara Frontier where their early historic occupation seems quite well founded.

The Wenro, Neutral, and Erie had each left the Niagara Frontier prior to 1655, the beginning of the second phase of the historic period. From that time on the area was frontier country for the Seneca. The power and territory of the League was rapidly expanding. Certainly the war parties of the other members of the League were making some use of the territory. It is impossible to state at present whether the Niagara Frontier was unoccupied for a time, just as there is some question whether the Erie villages of 1655 were still within the area. It is clear that the main Seneca villages were still in the Genesee country.

Houghton (1909: 283) claimed that there was a Seneca village at Youngstown as early as 1650, but I do not interpret the reference as he does. The first indisputable reference is that of Galinée (1917: 188-89) in 1669. Galinée's first information about the village came from a visitor in the Seneca village where he was stopping. He was told that there was a village of Five Nations Iroquois located for hunting at the west end of Lake Ontario. The Father proceeded there and upon arriving, learned that the name of the village was Ganastoqué Sonontoua Outinaouatoua. This seems to indicate that it was a Seneca village.

At this time, Galinée (1917: 176) mentioned that the Andaste were hunting on the edges of the Seneca country and were even coming close to the Seneca villages. The Andaste probably had no villages in the Niagara Frontier area, but may have slowed the Seneca expansion westward somewhat until their defeat in 1675. Hence, from at least 1669 to 1780 the Niagara Frontier was regarded as Seneca territory. In 1780, after the Seneca devastation by Sullivan, many of the Seneca from the main villages, located near Canandaigua Lake before their destruction, moved into the Niagara Frontier and soon settled on Tonawanda Creek and Buffalo Creek. This marks the beginning of the third phase of the historic period. Some Seneca may have moved into villages that already were in existence. Here they have remained, and many are still residents of the Tonawanda and Cattaraugus Reservations.

The documentary and cartographic evidence for the possible locations of the Neutral, Wenro, and Erie in the Niagara Frontier Region for the period 1615-55 has been presented. The ethnohistory of the subsequent period has been summarized. The conclusions were as follows:

1. The Neutral had several villages east of the Niagara River. They were probably close to the river and were occupied for a short time span, possibly from 1630-45.

2. The Wenro probably occupied part of the Niagara Frontier until 1638. Their location seems to have been somewhere between the Niagara River and the Genesee River.

3. The Erie occupied the Niagara Frontier from the general vicinity of Buffalo to Cattaraugus Creek. This may have been just prior to 1644. About this time they moved inland, and this may account for their next location farther south between Eighteenmile Creek and Chautauqua Lake. Questions about their location in the Allegheny drainage and in Ohio and Pennsylvania are left open.

4. The Neutral, Wenro, and Erie occupation of the Niagara Frontier had ceased by 1655. Shortly thereafter the Seneca started expanding into this area where many still remain.

It is obvious from the above discussion of the ethnohistory that no village of the early historic period can be satisfactorily documented. Because the areas of the Neutral, Wenro, and Erie may have overlapped at different periods of time, it is impossible at present to assign a particular site to one of these tribes on the basis of its location within a particular area. In the future it may be possible to do this under the following conditions:

1. More precise dating of historic sites from European trade material.

2. Excavation and identification of historic Neutral sites from west of the Niagara River.

3. Excavation and identification of certain sites in the Niagara Frontier as Neutral on the basis of similarity to the Ontario sites.

4. Excavation and study of sites in the Niagara Frontier which are not Neutral, under the hypothesis that there were two different groups of sites covering the same time period but geographically separated at any one time. These would represent the sites of the Wenro and Erie.

Conclusions from the ethnohistory have been of little value for the problem of establishing a chronological framework in the Niagara Frontier. Two of the seven sites under consideration, Goodyear and Green Lake, had European trade goods and must be assigned to the historic period. On the basis of kinds and amount of trade material, they predate the Seneca occupation of the area. This places them in the period from 1550-1655. They were undoubtedly villages of either the Neutral, Wenro, or Erie. But the difficulties of documenting any site of one of these groups precludes any more specific identification. Indeed it seems that in the Niagara Frontier archaeological evidence will be required to substantiate the early historic locations of these ethnic groups. For this reason, the sites to be used in establishing a chronological framework for the Niagara Frontier will be referred to only as "Iroquois" sites; for further distinction, archaeological rather than ethnic terminology will be used.

VI

HISTORY AND SELECTED FEATURES OF THE SITES

A chronological sequence for the pottery-producing village sites of the Niagara Frontier must at this time be based on comparative evidence from only those seven sites included in the hypothesis. Those sites are Oakfield, the earliest under the hypothesis, Kienuka, next later, Shelby, Buffam Street, and Eaton, all prehistoric and intermediate, and Goodyear and Green Lake, latest and of the historic period. Since reports on none of these sites have been published and the materials are widely scattered, it seems advisable to give here certain details on the history of these sites. A detailed list of the samples used and the locations of collections from each site is contained in Appendix C. Since the history of archaeological observations and excavations at each site provided the information for most of the attributes of settlement pattern and burial practices, these features will be included in the description of the sites.

The Oakfield Site

The Oakfield Site, Mda 1-4, the farthest east of the group, is located in the township of Oakfield, Genesee County. About half of the site is at present under cultivation by A. D. Martin of Oakfield who has leased the land for a number of years. This site was probably visited by Reverend Samuel Kirkland in 1788 (Squier, 1851: 65-68). Several later archaeologists have listed the site, but no large-scale excavating has been done (Beauchamp, 1900: 68; Houghton, 1909: 284; Parker, 1922: 561). Laverne Pechuman of Lockport has the largest collection of material from the site and has been carefully excavating there for some years (Pechuman, 1958). He has been most helpful in allowing the use of his collection, in making arrangements so that I could map and test on the site in 1954 for the New York State Science Service, and in discussing with me the material from the site.

The site is on the Huron Plain, about one mile north of the Onondaga Escarpment. It adjoins a small stream, part of the headwaters of one branch of Oak Orchard Creek. The topography is gently rolling and does not offer any defensive advantage. The soil along the creek is Fulton silty clay loam while that of the site and surrounding fields is Cazenovia silt loam, a soil with high productivity.

An earth embankment surrounded the area of the site and is still clearly visible on the uncultivated half (Squier, 1851: 65). This part of the site was mapped in 1954 by Charles Gillette of the New York State Museum, with my assistance. It was impossible at that time to determine the full extent of the ring. The area still enclosed by the earthwork is 2.9 acres. Estimates from Squier's map and my own observations of the total area at one time enclosed by the earthwork range from 5.2 acres to 7.6 acres, but I believe 5.2 is a closer approximation. Kirkland, on the other hand, estimated 4 acres (Squier, 1851: 66).

Squier and Houghton both mentioned the presence of a palisade, but presented no evidence (Squier, 1851: 65; Houghton, 1909: 364). Excavations made in 1958 by the writer disclosed several holes dug into the subsoil below the bank. These holes probably contained posts at one time. The excavated area was too limited in extent to exhibit any pattern in the distribution of these holes (White, 1959).

No concentrated midden area has been located on the site. The topsoil averages about 4 inches in thickness and in many places has eroded off completely, exposing the clay subsoil. Cultural debris is very scarce. The ditches outside the embankment, from which the soil was probably removed for the banks, have become partly filled with soil, some of which has eroded from the bank, the remainder of which may have been dumped refuse. Refuse has also been found in pits on the site.

The test trench in 1954 was dug for the purpose of investigating the number of components on the site. Typologically the material looked as if it might have been left by two different occupations. In the area excavated there was no indication of a stratigraphic separation. There was a concentration of cord-wrapped stick impressed pottery in the lower levels and a predominance of incised pottery in the top. The sample was small, and there was certainly an overlap of the two kinds of pottery. Pechuman also reports that he has been unable to observe any evidence of two occupations. Most of his material has been from pits in which a mixture of cord-wrapped stick impressed and incised pottery occurred from top to bottom. The shallowness of the topsoil and the scarcity of cultural material restrict excavation to disturbed areas such as pits and thus render very difficult a satisfactory solution of the problem of multiple occupations. In the absence of evidence to the contrary and because of certain typological evidence, the material from this site will be treated as if it were the remains of a single occupation.

Burials are reported by hearsay to have been dug between the earthworks and the gypsum plant, about one-half mile to the west. Benedict located three human vertebrae found by some unknown party at an unknown time. Each vertebrum had been pierced by an arrowpoint (exhibit and label in Buffalo Historical Society, "Burial place near prehistoric earthwork at Oakfield. Finder reports all from the same skeleton."). Houghton reported a human vertebrum which contained an arrowpoint found "by U.S. Gypsum Co." in a collection from the Oakfield site which he examined (unpublished notes in Buffalo Museum of Science).

The "Bone Fort" is reported in connection with this site. Neither the accounts nor the location are clear. My interpretation of Yates and

Moulton's account (1824: 16-17) of Kirkland's visit in 1788 is that the Oakfield Site is the southern of the two forts he saw. Kirkland claimed that the second, northern fort, was approximately two miles from the Oakfield Site and the "Bone Fort" was nearby. Squier changed northern to western and interpreted this as indicating the Oakfield Site and, therefore, located the "Bone Fort" a mile northeast. This was described as a mound 6 feet high and 30 feet in diameter at the base (Squier, 1851: 66-67). Squier's description of the contents bears the most resemblance to an ossuary. If this is a correct interpretation, the ossuary might have been connected with the Oakfield Site since a mile is not an unusual distance for the location of an ossuary from a village. On the other hand, there is no longer any evidence for the existence of a "Bone Fort."

The Kienuka Site

The Kienuka Site, Twa 1-1, lies on the edge of the Niagara Escarpment, immediately adjacent to the Tuscarora Indian Reservation, on the property of Cameron Nicholson, in the township of Lewiston, Niagara County. Like the other sites, it has been known for a long time and numerous people have visited and excavated here. It has been mentioned by Cusick (1825: 29), Schoolcraft (1847: 209), Johnson (1881: 173-85), Thomas (1891: 512-13), Beauchamp (1900: 107-8), Houghton (1909: 322), Parker (1922: 632), and MacNeish (1952: 11). Richard McCarthy, Ralph Ward, and Beverly Ward of Lockport have been working on the site for a number of years.

There were at least three occupations on the site, of which two were historic and one prehistoric. One of the historic occupations is indicated by extensive European trade goods, such as scissors and thimbles, found on the surface. These are probably the remains of a village of the Revolutionary Period (information from McCarthy). The second occupation is represented by an ossuary, opened in 1904 by Peter Porter and later reopened by McCarthy (information from McCarthy). This produced early European trade goods as well as native artifacts. MacNeish (1952: 11) has dated the ossuary in the first half of the seventeenth century. The third occupation is prehistoric and is the only one which will be considered further here.

The site itself lies on the north edge of the Huron Plain, and the northern edge of the site is formed by the Niagara Escarpment (Fig. 7). Through the southern part of the site flows Tuscarora Creek, part of the headwaters of Twelvemile Creek. The prehistoric cultural material is concentrated in a midden area just north of this small creek. Cultural debris from all occupations covers an area of about 5.5 acres, but this was probably not the extent of the early occupation.

The soil on top of the escarpment is Dunkirk silty loam and Ontario loam. The latter is especially productive. The soil below the escarpment is Lockport silty loam, poorly drained and of low productivity.

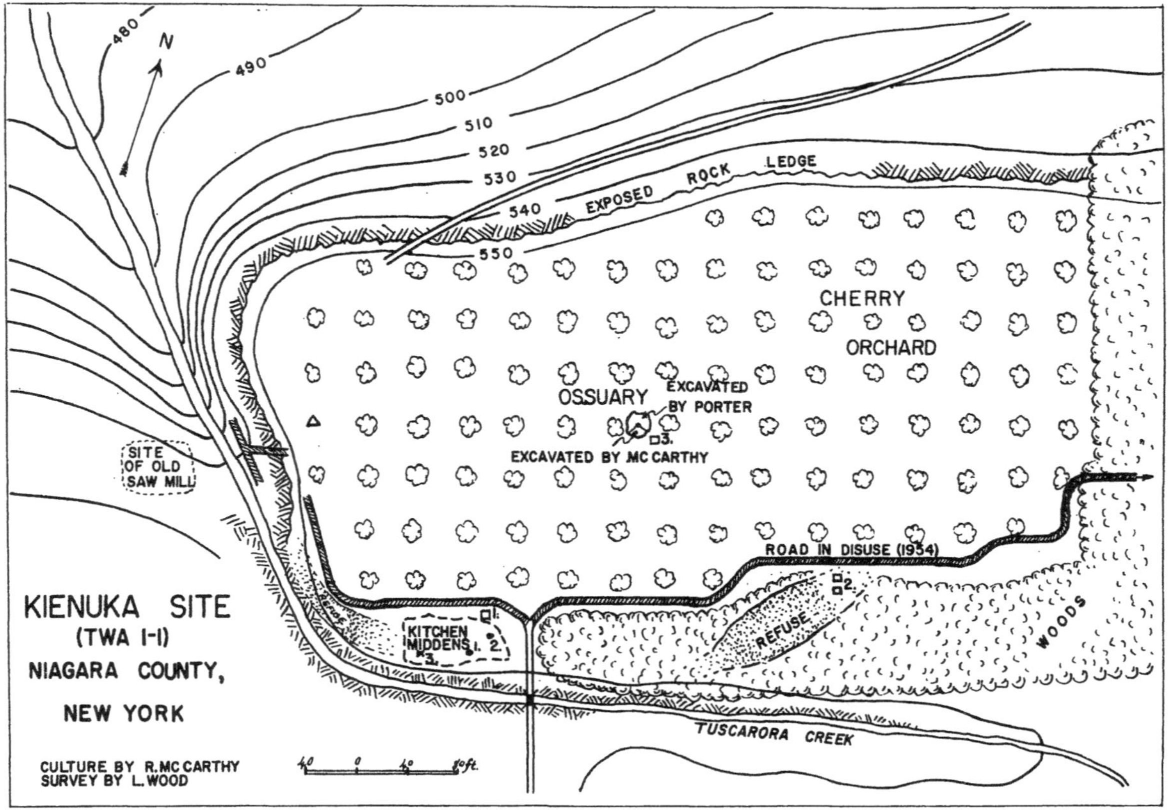

Fig. 7. Map of the Kienuka Site.

The position of the site might be advantageous for defense since the north and part of the west sides are formed by the escarpment rising abruptly about 70 feet above the Ontario Plain. The site probably had an earth embankment, but no evidence has been visible for some time. Houghton (1909: 322) wrote as if he had observed the embankment.

There were two mounds on or near the site (Turner, 1849: 26; Houghton, 1909: 322). Beauchamp (1900: 107-8) reviewed the evidence for these features but reached no conclusions. Several ossuaries are associated with the site and some of these may be the mounds to which reference has been made. One ossuary of the contact period located on the site has already been mentioned. Three more were west of the site. Thomas dug one of these and reported that it consisted of a low mound, 1.5 feet high. This contained numerous skeletons as well as three copper rings (Thomas, 1891: 513). It clearly is related to one of the later occupations. Thomas opened two more ossuaries only enough to determine that they contained skeletons. It is impossible to determine whether these are related to the early, prehistoric occupation.

The Shelby Site

The Shelby Site, Mda 2-1, is 11 miles northwest of the Oakfield Site in the township of Shelby, Orleans County, near a small branch of Johnson's Creek. The site was reported by Squier (1851: 71-72), but he did not visit it. Cushing (1875: 377) gave an account of it and mentioned the artifacts found there in great numbers. Beauchamp (1900: 132) published a sketch map and first pointed out that the site was Iroquois. Parker (1922: 632) later suggested that it might be Neutral.

This site, also on the Huron Plain, is surrounded by a double earth wall in the form of a circle. These features are shown in Figure 8. Approximately 3.5 acres are enclosed by the walls. A test trench was dug through the banks by the Anthropology Section of the Buffalo Museum under the direction of McCarthy. This excavation did not disclose any post molds. Several more test trenches should probably be dug before the problem of a palisade is settled. There was no midden area outside the rings, but several areas within produced a concentration of refuse. McCarthy has also found pits within the enclosure. The site is located on level ground, near a swamp which has nearly dried up in recent years. In 1875, when Cushing (1875: 376) published his account of the site, the swamp was 10 rods south of the works, and he felt that the swamp had been a shallow lake at one time. Headwaters of both Johnson's Creek and Oak Orchard Creek start in the swamp. There are three kinds of soil nearby, Honeoye silt loam, Lyons loam, and muck. The first is preferable for general farm crops.

Robert Hill of Rochester removed about thirty burials from the site in recent years. The position of some is given on the map (information from McCarthy). Grave goods were very scarce, their occurrence

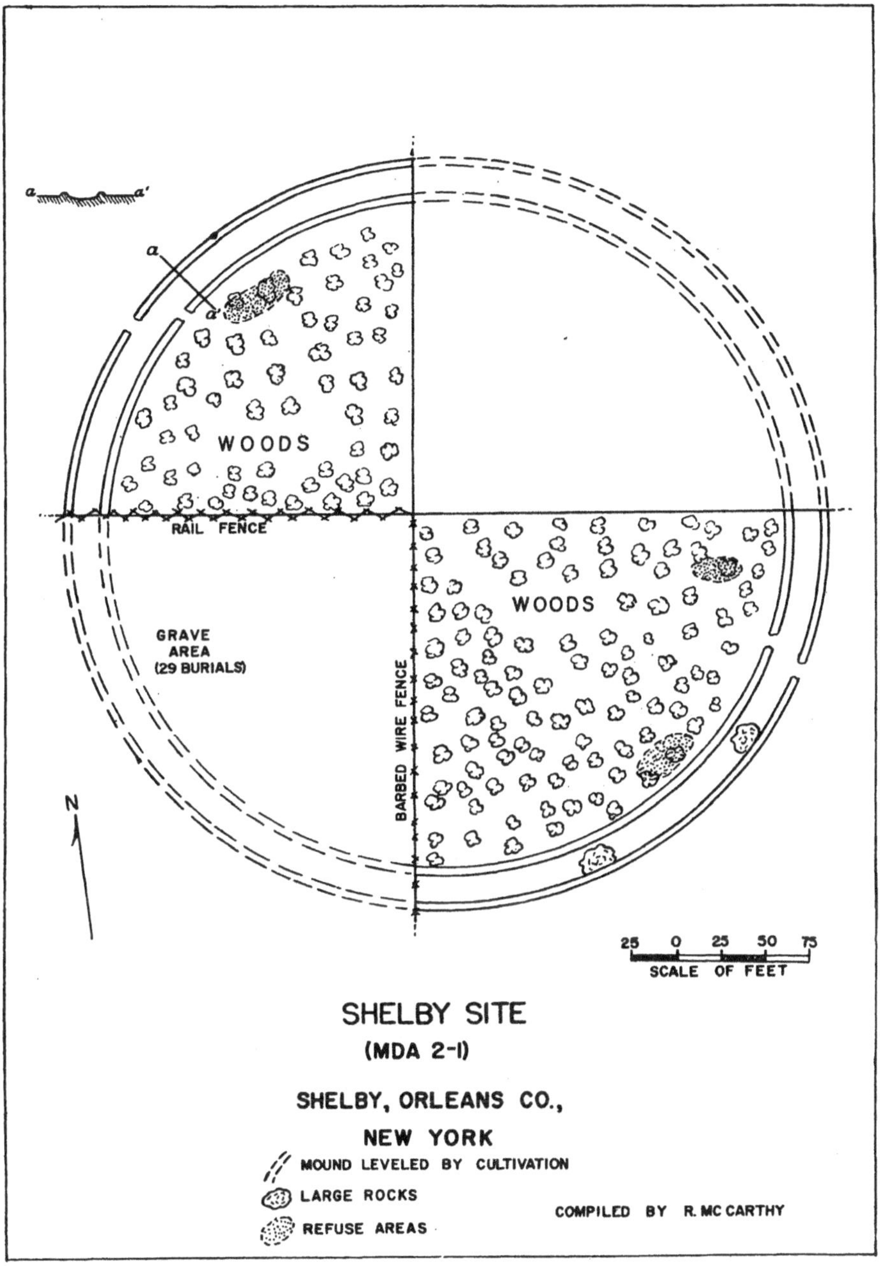

Fig. 8. Map of the Shelby Site.

being noted by McCarthy in only one instance, when a single shell bead was found (information from McCarthy who obtained it from Hill). In addition to the cemetery, Squier (1851: 72) and Cushing (1875: 376) both mention a "Bone Pit" 1.5 miles away. This suggests an ossuary but there are no data available on what was found or the possible connection with the Shelby Site.

The Buffam Street Site

The Buffam Street or Buffam (Buffum) Site, Buf 3-4, is in the southern part of the city of Buffalo, less than a mile from Buffalo Creek to the north and Cazenovia Creek to the south. It is also known locally as the "Indian Cemetery," "Indian Church Road Site," and "Old Indian Burying Ground." Squier (1851: 72-75) mapped the area at a time when the Buffalo Creek Seneca's cemetery was still standing at one end of the area occupied by an older village of Indians. Schoolcraft (1847: 213-18) also visited and sketched the site.

Late in the nineteenth century the Seneca burials were moved to Forest Lawn Cemetery, Buffalo, and excavation was begun on the middens of the earlier village. Houghton, Benedict, and Imogene Strickler Robertson dug the major part of three middens, and at that time there was a large body of material. Some of the digging was done in 1894 and again in 1897 and 1898. Houghton's research was sponsored by the Buffalo Society of Natural Sciences, and the material was turned over to the Buffalo Museum of Science. Benedict's Collection was presented to the Buffalo Historical Society where MacNeish studied it in the late 1940's. The Robertson Collection has been kept intact by her family and is still in their possession in Buffalo. Some sherds from this site were found in the Ceramic Repository of The University of Michigan and were originally probably part of the Houghton Collection.

MacNeish (1952: 22), on the basis of typology and a rather unspecific location on a Delisle map which has been mentioned previously (p. 35), considered this site to be historical Neutral and therefore used it as the historic component for establishing the Neutral-Wenro sequence. The early occupation of this village, however, contained no European trade goods to my knowledge. The three collections which I examined contained none. In addition, there are explicit statements to this effect by two of the early excavators (Houghton, 1899: 3; 1909: 343; Robertson, 1952: 23-29). The site itself is located on the Erie Plain. A large part of it is still preserved beneath a small city park, built in memory of the historic Seneca graves which were intrusive on the earlier site. When Squier (1851: 73-75) and Schoolcraft (1847: 218) independently mapped the site, each noted an embankment surrounding it. This is shown in Figure 9, adapted from sketches in Squier and Robertson. Houghton (1920: 17) has accepted the presence of the earth embankment and also Squier's (1851: 73-75) statement that a palisade existed. There is no evidence cited for the latter.

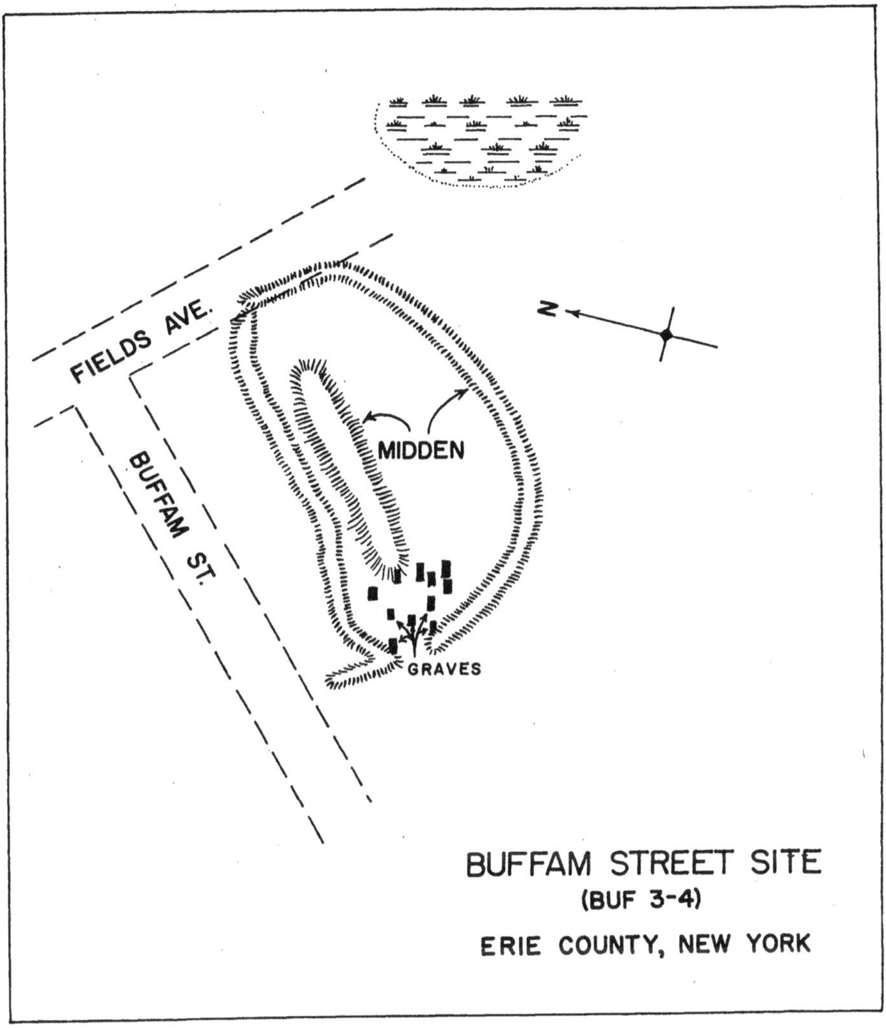

Fig. 9. Map of the Buffam Street Site.

The site probably was not selected for an easily defended position (Houghton, 1909: 15). Squier (1851: 73) estimated that the area enclosed by the earthwork was about four acres. He gives no scale on his map, but if the scale here is consistent with that on a number of his other maps, my estimate is 3.2 acres. The site was on a sandy terrace of Buffalo Creek which is now about .6 miles north. This terrace rises 20 to 30 feet above the flats and has a gentle slope down to them. At the foot of the terrace on the north is a swampy area, where formerly there were springs (Squier, 1851: 74). There is no direct evidence of the soil type, but the site is in an area characterized by Fulton silt loam, as is the Eaton Site.

Five middens were visible when the site was under cultivation (Robertson, 1952: 24). The approximate position of two middens has been indicated on the map. Therefore, the material which I examined came from three separate middens, since Houghton, Benedict, and Robertson each excavated in a different midden (Robertson, 1952: 24-25). The cemetery was located a few hundred feet to the north on a sandy knoll (Houghton, 1920: 20). Grave goods were rare. The graves shown in Figure 9 were Seneca burials of the Buffalo Creek Reservation period.

A mound, or possibly two mounds, are mentioned in connection with the site. Squier located one a short distance from the site, and Houghton (1909: 312) connected this with a mound which he excavated on Armine Street, about .8 miles away. Schoolcraft mentioned a mound within the earthworks and located it on his map. In his excavations of part of the mound he found bone fragments and pottery (Schoolcraft, 1847: 216-17). It is impossible to tell whether this mound was connected with the Iroquois occupation. Tradition (Turner, 1849: 30) has identified the mound as the final resting place of those who were slaughtered in the last battle between the Kahkwas and the Seneca.

The Eaton Site

Approximately 1.5 miles southeast of the last site is the Eaton Site, Buf 2-4. The eastern part of this is on the property owned by Will and Donald Eaton, West Seneca, while the western portion is on the property of Stanley Nikiel of Buffalo. Will Eaton was most helpful in telling me the history of the site and pointing out the areas where past work has been done. He also stated that in the years of cultivating the field occupied by the site he had never found European trade goods. Although this site has been known locally for a long time, it received very little attention in the literature until the survey of Houghton (1909: 310-11). Parker (1922: 551) also listed the site.

This site is also on the Erie Plain and is immediately adjacent to Cazenovia Creek. Here an oval knoll rises nearly 30 feet above the surrounding land. The total area of the knoll which is suitable for occupation is approximately 2.2 acres. This estimate was obtained from a map of the site made in 1954 by Charles Gillette of the New York State Museum and the writer. The limits of occupation are unknown. On the south and west the bank falls away sharply to the creek flats. On the other side it falls away more gradually. The soil of the northern part of the site and surrounding area is Genesee silt loam, a highly productive soil. Toward the creek is Fulton silt loam, of lower productivity.

No earth embankment has ever been reported. Since Squier apparently did a thorough job of investigating the earthworks in the area and was only 1.5 miles away at Buffam Street, it seems likely that he would have reported one from Eaton, if such had existed. The site would have been quite well protected on two sides by the steep banks. The surface of the occupied area has been under cultivation for many years and at present yields few signs of occupation. There were probably extensive hillside middens on the banks at one time. Most of them have eroded away, partly as a result of previous careless digging. The burials from this site have never been located, nor have European trade goods been found on the site (Houghton, 1909: 318; 1920: 17).

The Goodyear Site

The Goodyear Site, Dep 1-4, is in the township of Elma, Erie County, on property formerly owned by the Goodyear family and managed by George Goodyear of Buffalo. It was at one time known locally as the Mullen Site. This site was first reported by Charles Simmons of East Elma to Houghton (1909: 315) and was later listed by Parker (1922: 552). I have excavated on this site for short periods from 1948 to 1951, together with other interested local people, most of whom were members of the Anthropology Section of the Buffalo Museum of Science. The following were regular workers: Virginia Cummings, Alene Dickinson, Richard McCarthy, Ralph and Beverly Ward, Betts Albro, Norma Emigh, and Ruth Schmidt.

This site is located toward the south of the Erie Plain on a bluff formed by the old valley of Buffalo Creek. The creek is now .3 of a mile west. The site is well protected by banks on three sides and by two knolls on the fourth. The north and south ravines have been cut by small branches of Buffalo Creek and are somewhat shallower than the creek valley on the west. The latter drops about 50 feet below the level of the site. The soil, Genesee silt loam, adjoins the creek while farther back, the flats are of Fulton silt loam. The site and the surrounding fields are of Cazenovia silt loam. The first and the last of these soils are highly productive. This is a large site with approximately 5.7 acres covered by occupational debris. It still shows abundant evidence of occupation. There were extensive hillside middens on three sides. The surface at plowing still shows seven large oval dark areas, probably associated with house structures and living debris. Several refuse-filled pits have also been found.

Extensive testing disclosed only three graves. It seems doubtful that these were part of any sizable cemetery in this area. Two of the three graves contained grave goods, including a circular oval pendant of European brass. On the surface several brass bangles and scraps of kettles have been found, as well as iron axes. Only two fragments of metal appeared in the midden excavations. No European trade beads were found on the surface in my numerous collecting trips. Three trade beads are in the Reed Collection. Two are blue beads, the third a melon bead with blue background and a white stripe, bordered by red (Kidd, in Ritchie, 1954: 38-43). Both types are present on the earliest sites of the Seneca sequence, the Adams and Tram Sites, dated 1550-75 (Wray and Schoff, 1953: 55, 63). These bead types cover a considerable time span and are not useful in dating the site.

The Green Lake Site

The Green Lake Site, Buf 1-4, was excavated in 1929 by William A. Ritchie for the Rochester Museum of Arts and Sciences. It is located in the township of Orchard Park, Erie County, on the Erie Plain. The site originally lay on the bank of a small tributary of Smoke Creek which was later dammed up to form Green Lake. When Ritchie dug the site in 1929, the lake had covered a portion of it. In the unpublished notes of Reed at the Buffalo Museum of Science there is the statement that an iron knife was found "where ground over fireplaces was scraped off to form Green Lake." Because it is impossible to know how much of the area of occupation was destroyed, estimates of the size of the site may be quite inaccurate. My estimate from Ritchie's map (Fig. 10) is 3 to 5 acres.

Nearby soils are Chenango silt loam, Chagrin silt loam, both moderate to high in productivity, and Wooster gravelly loam. The terrain slopes rather gradually down to the lake, and the position would not seem to be one selected for defense. There is no report of an earth ring. The middens which Ritchie dug were on the southern slope but were not thick, hillside middens.

At least eleven burials have been found on the site, but there is little additional information on them (information gathered by Ritchie and contained in his field notes). A statement by Houghton (1920: 22) says: "A few European articles have been found in its graves." The general digging on the site has also produced European trade goods but not in large quantities. Two rolled brass beads were found by the Rochester Museum party. The Reed Collection contains the following: pea-sized blue glass trade bead, iron celt, three iron awls, three rolled brass beads, rolled brass earring, and two iron knives (mentioned in notes only).

Summary

Information on the location, history of excavation, and features of settlement pattern and burial practices has been presented for each of the seven sites under consideration. These data have been summarized in Table I. Certain of them will be treated comparatively in a later section.

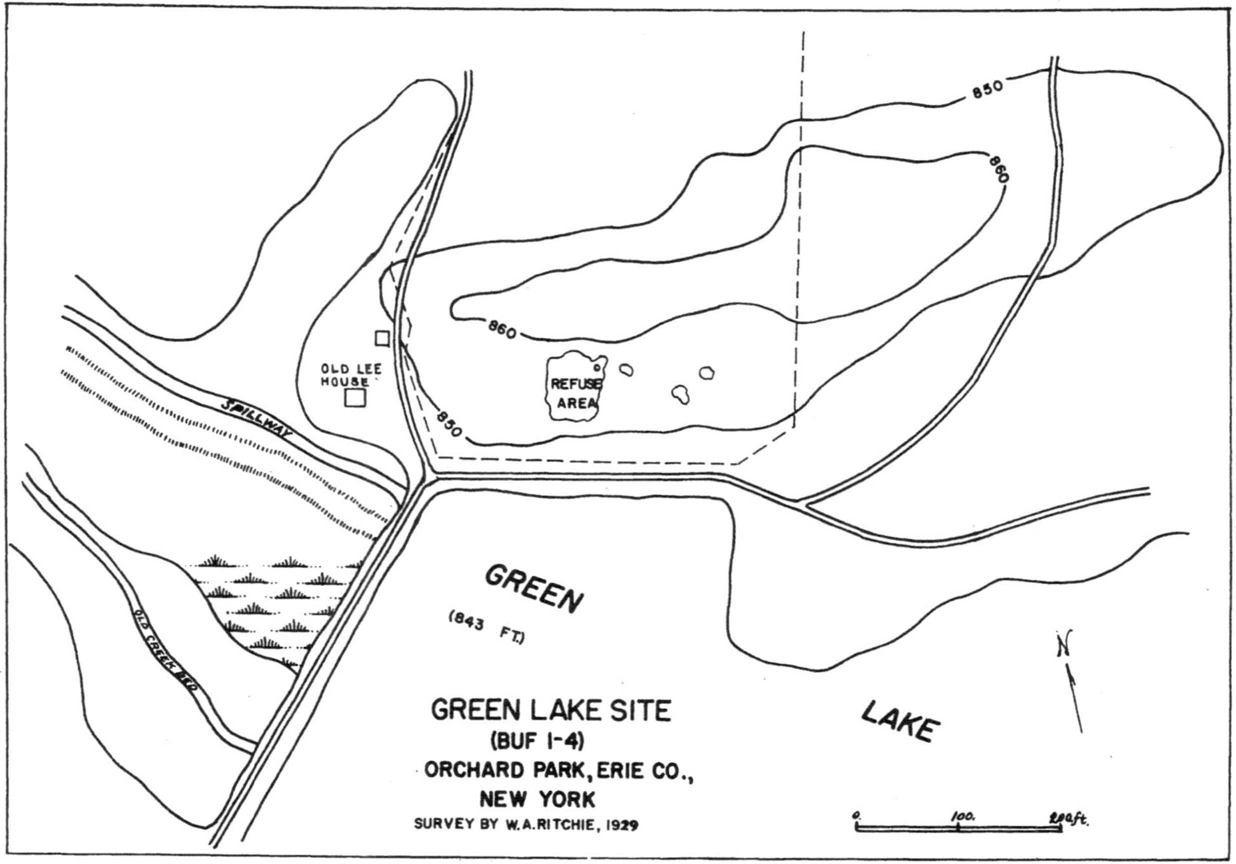

Fig. 10. Map of the Green Lake Site.

TABLE I

ATTRIBUTES OF SETTLEMENT PATTERN AND BURIAL PRACTICES

Attribute	Site*						
	GL	G	E	B	S	K	O
Size of site (acres). . . .	3-5	5-7	2.2	3-4	3.7	. . .	5
On Huron Plain	. . .	. . .	. . .	. . .	x	x	x
On Erie Plain	x	x	x	x	. . .	. . .	. . .
Near headwaters	x	. . .	. . .	. . .	x	x	x
Near main stream	. . .	x	x	x	. . .	. . .	. . .
Alluvial loam	x	x	x	?	. . .	. . .	. . .
Grey-brown podzol loam	. . .	x	x	?	x	x	x
Defensible position. . . .	. . .	x	x	. . .	. . .	x	. . .
Earth embankment	. . .	. . .	. . .	x	x	?	x
Hillside midden	. . .	x	x	. . .	. . .	. . .	. . .
Individual burials.	x	x	. . .	x	x	. . .	x
Ossuary	. . .	. . .	. . .	. . .	?	?	?
Grave goods common . .	x	x	. . .	. . .	. . .	. . .	. . .
European trade goods . .	x	x	. . .	. . .	. . .	. . .	. . .

Note: — x indicates presence of the attribute. ? indicates probable presence but better evidence required.

*In all tables the site name will be abbreviated by using the first letter of the name, except GL for Green Lake.

VII

ARCHAEOLOGICAL DATA

In the preceding sections the problem of establishing the chronological framework for seven pottery-producing sites in the Niagara Frontier has been stated, and the procedure and assumptions have been discussed. A hypothesis has been advanced which includes alternate arrangements of the seven sites in temporal order from the latest to the earliest. This hypothesis will now be tested by presenting the archaeological data as evidence for choosing among these arrangements.

The data from each site will be compared to those from the other sites to show the similarities and differences existing among the sites. These similarities will be measured in terms of the likeness of certain selected attributes of the archaeological data. An ordering of the sites from the similarities of each attribute considered independently will allow the selection of the best arrangement of sites according to that attribute. Each best arrangement will be examined to see whether it can be considered to be the result of temporal differences, i.e., to see whether it conforms to one of the arrangements of the hypothesis. In this way, evidence will be accumulated independently in support of the one arrangement which allows the inference of the chronological order of the sites from late to early.

The attributes of the archaeological data which have been selected for study and which will be presented in the following order pertain to these classes of artifacts and features, pottery, projectile points, pipes, settlement pattern, and burial practices. The data for each attribute will be presented in this order, Green Lake, Goodyear, Eaton, Buffam, Shelby, Kienuka, and Oakfield.

Pottery

Ceramic attributes, studied for their clues to chronological relations, may be divided into three groups: (1) those which show a consistent trend toward increasing or decreasing frequency for all sites considered and thus are useful for inferring chronology, (2) those which are restricted in their distribution to certain sites and thus are useful for inferring the chronological relationships among only those sites, and (3) those which do not show a consistent trend or a restricted distribution and thus may represent local stylistic differences.

An example of an attribute of the first group which MacNeish (1952: 82) recognized in his study of Iroquois pottery types is that of incised decoration. Incising in Iroquois ceramics shows an increasing popularity from early to late. In contrast to this, the technique of interrupted linear decoration occurs only at certain sites and is regarded as a time marker of late Owasco and early Iroquois (MacNeish, 1952: 19). In this instance, the attribute of interrupted linear decoration is an attribute of Group 2. Finally, the attribute of notches across the lip, perpendicular to the long axis of the lip, on pottery vessels from the seven sites considered here has a popularity ranging from 14 per cent at one site to 1 per cent at another. The ranking of the seven sites by the similarities of the popularity of this attribute in no way conforms to any of the arrangements of the hypothesis. Therefore one must conclude that this attribute had a fluctuating popularity which was unrelated to a temporal trend and which requires further interpretation.

It should be emphasized that the assignment of a particular attribute to one of the above groups will vary with the data at hand and is a conclusion from a study of the data rather than an *a priore* classification. For example, the attribute of interrupted linear technique would not be assigned to the second group unless the data included some sites at which this technique was a time marker. On the other hand, if all the sites in a study produced interrupted linear pottery, it might be treated as an attribute of Group 1 or Group 3, depending upon whether changes in frequency were orderly, and the order one which allowed chronological inferences.

The third group of attributes, then, is a catchall for those attributes which can not be shown to belong to Group 1 or Group 2. Ideally, the popularity of these Group 3 attributes could be ascribed to local (site) stylistic differences. In practice, many of the differences in the popularity of the attributes of Group 3 are so slight from site to site that they may result from sampling error. Since these attributes of Group 3 were not useful for this study, no explanation of the differences will be made in most instances.

Each attribute of Group 1 will be treated as part of an attribute class to show the ordering of the data and the implications for the temporal relations among the sites. These attribute classes are: (1) collared and uncollared vessels, (2) rim decoration, and (3) rim profile. The attribute class presentations will be followed by a summary and conclusions about the chronological order of the sites from the evidence of the attribute classes of Group 1. The attribute classes of Group 2 will follow. Each of these nine attribute classes will be examined to see its bearing on the conclusions reached from the study of the Group 1 data. A summary will present the conclusion from the evidence of the attributes of Group 1 and Group 2. Certain attributes of Group 3 will be mentioned briefly, only to the extent that they are deemed important for past or future studies.

In selecting and defining the attributes of each of the three groups which follow, various classifications have been tried. Only that classification which allowed the best order in terms of one of the alternatives of the hypothesis will be presented. "Best" as here defined is that arrangement which deviates least from the desired arrangement, one in which there is an orderly progression in the comparative factors (Robinson, 1951: 300). In order to arrive at the best arrangement for each attribute class, it has been necessary to eliminate certain categories for some classes and combine other categories. For example, undecorated vessels were not included in examining similarities of techniques of decoration. Circular and oval punctations were combined in a consideration of the attribute class of additional rim decoration in a second example. If at first glance this procedure appears arbitrary, this is only because the classifications and subsequent orderings which have been discarded in favor of the best arrangement are not here presented. In other words, the classifications used here have been selected because they yielded differences which were systematic and consequently useful in testing the hypothesis about the chronological relationship of the sites (Brainerd, 1951: 305).

The evidence which led to the final selection of the best ordering of the comparative factors is not presented in detail. The conclusion, i.e., the best arrangement of the data for each attribute class, together with a statement of how much the best arrangement differs from the ideal arrangement (Robinson, 1951: 301), is given for each attribute class considered.

Attribute Classes of Group 1

Collared and Uncollared Vessels. — The attribute of collared vessels compared to that of vessels without collars was in general a clearcut, easily recognizable distinction. By definition a collar was any noticeable thickening on the external surface of the rim area (Fig. 11). There were a few instances in which it was difficult to distinguish between a squared, thickened lip and a very narrow collar. Such vessels were classified as collared unless there was decoration below the squared area which would indicate that the latter was being treated as a lip while the area below was decorated as a rim.

A group of twenty-seven vessels from Shelby presented a problem in classification. All of these had a wide decorated area, and many of them had broken in such a way that the bottom of this decorated area was missing. Sherds of this approximate size from the other sites would generally have shown a complete rim area.

Some of these rims showed a slight thickening toward the bottom of the decorated area while others showed no thickening. Still others were incomplete, making an observation of thickness indicative of a collar impossible. On the basis of other similarities between the complete rims and the incomplete rims, I judged that these twenty-seven vessels should be treated as a group and that the omission of the numerous incomplete ones would have introduced a bias into the sample. Even though the slight thickening on some might have been regarded as an incipient collar (Fig. 11), it was decided to treat the group as if it were uncollared. To be consistent, three vessels from the Buffam Street Site

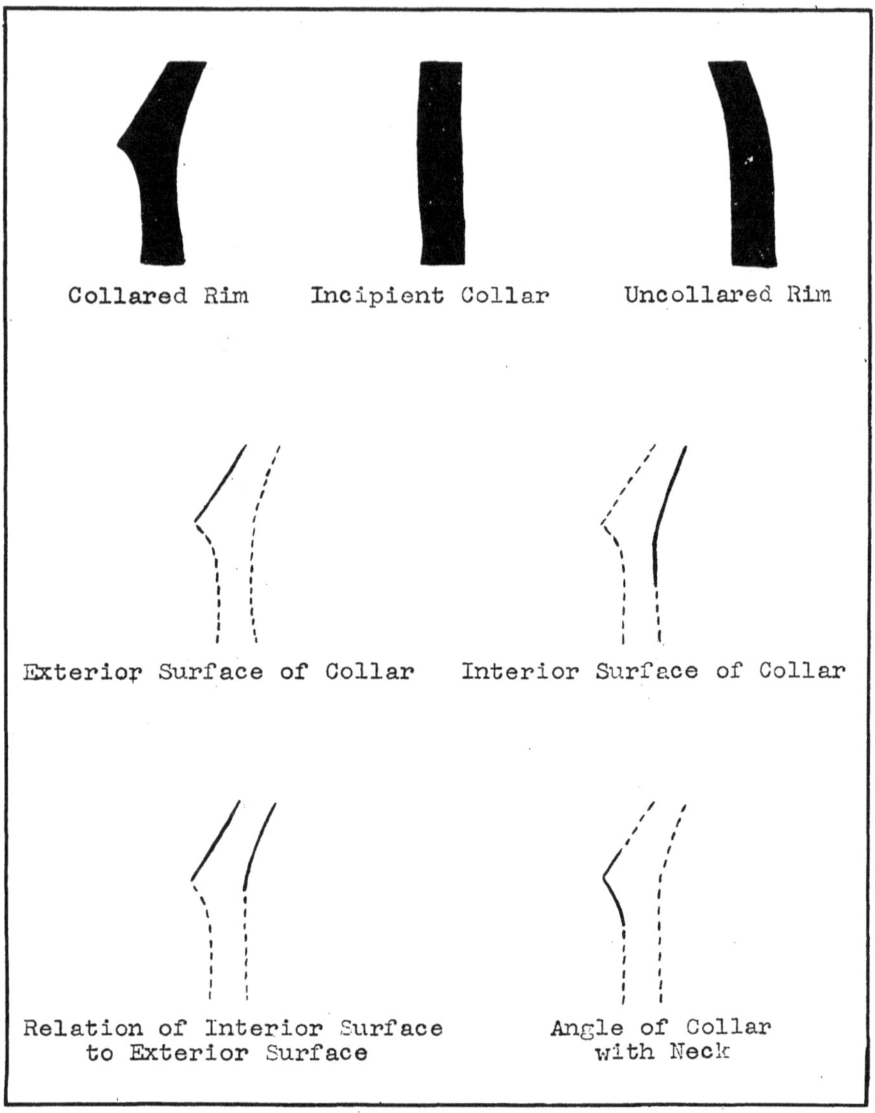

Fig. 11. Attributes of Rim Profiles.

with similar slight thickening were also classified as uncollared. The frequency of collared vessels compared to uncollared vessels at each site is given in Table II.

The best arrangement of the sites based on differences in the frequencies of collared vessels is: Green Lake, Goodyear, Eaton, Buffam, Shelby, Kienuka, and Oakfield. This arrangement of the coefficients of

TABLE II

FREQUENCY OF COLLARED AND UNCOLLARED VESSELS

Site	Number of Vessels Represented		
	Collared	Uncollared	Total
Green Lake.	254	21	275
Goodyear	364	43	407
Eaton.	78	9	87
Buffam.	113	15	128
Shelby	191	41	232
Kienuka	104	27	131
Oakfield	90	29	119

agreement departs from the ideal arrangement by .3 per cent. This ordering of the sites may be considered a chronological one since it is one of those presented in the hypothesis as possible chronological arrangements.

The measure between the best arrangement of the coefficients of agreement and the ideal arrangement, in this case .3 per cent, is computed following Robinson's (1951: 300) method. When arranging the coefficients of agreement in order of decreasing frequency from a left to right diagonal, certain individual coefficients do not demonstrate this decreasing order. These coefficients which deviate from the desired order can be designated by a minus sign. For example, in a series of coefficients of agreement, 50, 40, 30, -35, 20, 10, the coefficient 35 would be preceded by a minus sign. The measure of the conformity of such an arrangement to the ideal arrangement (50, 40, 35, 30, 20, 10) would be obtained as follows: "We square all the negative differences, and then express the sum of these squares as a fraction of the sum of the squares of all differences, positive and negative together (Robinson, 1951: 300)." The negative difference in the above example is 5. The list of all differences is 10, 10, 5, 15, and 10. When the differences have been squared, the numerator is 25, and the denominator is 550, or 4.5 per cent. The arrangement of coefficients in the above example departs from the ideal arrangement by 4.5 per cent.

This measure of the amount by which a given arrangement differs from the ideal arrangement serves as one means of selecting the best arrangement from others which are similar.

Rim Decoration. — The decoration on the rims of pottery vessels was recorded by the motif or design of the decoration and by the technique used in executing the decoration. Motif referred only to the major design on the rim. This definition was further limited by restricting motif to decoration executed by a single technique. For example, if the decoration consisted of parallel lines incised obliquely, this alone was considered to be the motif, regardless of additional decoration such as a row of punctations beneath or notches at the junction of the rim and lip (Pl. III, Fig. 5 and 6). On the other hand, if the parallel incised oblique lines on the rim were underlined by an incised line, the whole was considered to be the motif (Pl. IV, Fig. 2).

Some difficulty was encountered with this definition when recording the pottery from the Oakfield Site. Here two or more techniques were sometimes used in executing a motif which was identical to one made by a single technique on the other sites. In these cases, the motif was defined by its similarity to a motif already recognized from the other sites. For example, the motif of parallel horizontal lines, executed partly by incising and partly by an interrupted linear technique was considered to be the same motif as parallel horizontal lines executed solely by an incised technique. On the other hand, when technique was considered, these were distinguished.

The following techniques were distinguished (Pl. 1):

1. Cord-wrapped stick impressed
2. Interrupted linear, linear punch or push and pull
3. Incised
4. Punctated
5. Plain or undecorated
6. Other

Since it was not clear whether undecorated vessels should be included as a category in comparing the popularity of techniques, I first compared each pair of sites on the basis of vessels with decorated rims and vessels with undecorated rims. The coefficients of agreement for decorated rims did not produce a systematic order from which chronology could be inferred. Therefore, the category of undecorated vessels was eliminated, and the total used was the number of vessels having decoration. The comparisons were based on five categories of techniques, (1) cord-wrapped stick impressed, (2) interrupted linear and linear punch, (3) incised, (4) punctated, and (5) other. "Other" includes unrecognizable techniques, as well as dentate stamping at Oakfield. Coefficients of agreement were computed and these were ordered by Robinson's method. The frequencies are shown in Table III.

The best arrangement is: Green Lake, Goodyear, Eaton, Buffam, Shelby, Kienuka, and Oakfield. This arrangement departs from the ideal arrangement by 1.4 per cent. The order of the sites based on comparisons of the attribute class of techniques of decoration is considered to result from temporal differences.

The rim decoration was classified into sixteen different motifs and later reduced to thirteen. Figure 12 shows those which were combined as well as those which were not. Each motif either occurred on at least two sites or, in the case of Numbers 10 and 11, is known to be a popular Iroquois motif from another area. My definition of motif did not include decoration below the collar, or on the neck of collarless vessels, or decoration made by any technique except the dominant technique of the

TABLE III

FREQUENCY OF TECHNIQUES OF RIM DECORATION

Techniques of Decoration	Number of Vessels Represented						
	Site						
	GL	G	E	B	S	K	O
Cord-wrapped stick	. .	. .	. .	. .	. .	. .	21
Interrupted linear	. .	. .	. .	. .	. .	12	17
Incised.	207	284	68	117	219	87	63
Punctated	29	35	3	5	6	19	6
Other.	8	2	2	1	1	9	16
Total.	244	321	'73	123	226	127	123

motif. At Oakfield there are exceptions to this last, as previously mentioned.

Motifs 1, 2, and 3 differ only in the direction of the incising (Pl. II, Figs. 1, 2, and 3). MacNeish (1952: 14) combined these in his pottery types. I did not combine them because it seemed necessary to use all possible differences in order to compare Green Lake, Goodyear, Eaton, and Buffam Street, all of which by inspection had very similar pottery. If these motifs had been combined, the greatest difference between any pair of these four sites, when compared for Motifs 1, 2, and 3 together, would have been 15 per cent.

Motifs 4 and 5 are very similar and might have been combined. But since MacNeish did not record Motif 5 in his work in other Iroquois areas, it seemed that this motif might be useful for differentiating the pottery of the Niagara Frontier from that of surrounding areas. This may prove to be the case, but because of its relative lack of popularity, its usefulness is limited.

Motif 6 was originally recorded as three motifs (Fig. 12, Motif 6, *a*, *b*, and *c*). The difference between (*a*) and (*b*) seemed to be frequently a matter of the size of the rim sherd, and I was unable to distinguish between them. (compare Pl. II, Figs. 4 and 5). Motif 6, (*b*), probably occurred as part of two distinct decorations. On some vessels it was found at the midpoint of the sides of the rim, where the dominant motifs on the vessel were 1 and 3, with 6 resulting from the change from 1 to 3 or vice versa. On other vessels, 6 (*b*) was repeated as a motif and in these cases, it differed from 6 (*c*) very little. The difference between 6 (*b*) and 6 (*c*) in these last cases may have been related to the width of collar, since it might have been difficult to execute 6 (*c*) on a very narrow collar. But even though these differences may occur, the nature of the data made it impossible to present evidence for them. Therefore, the three, 6 (*a*), (*b*), and (*c*), were combined.

Motif 7 was also recorded as two classes. Only the Green Lake Site

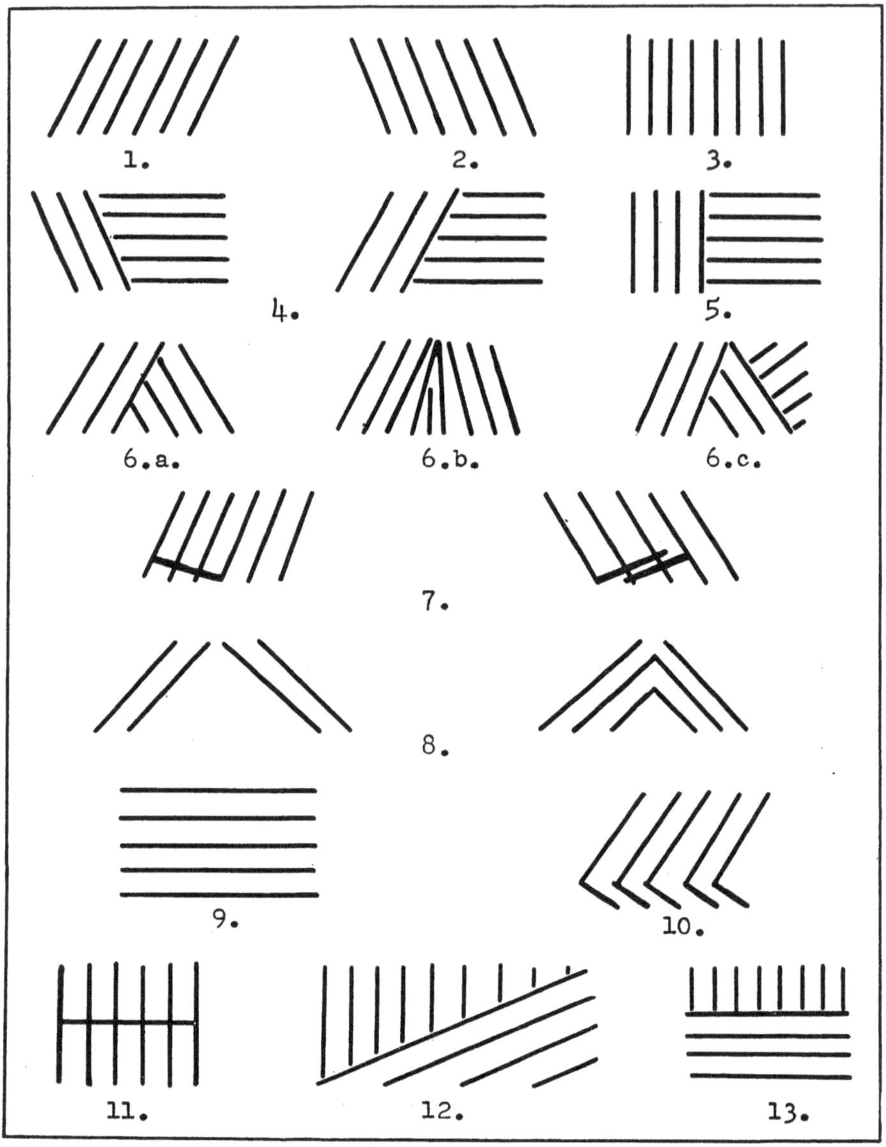

Fig. 12. Motifs of Decoration on Pottery Vessel Rims.

pottery showed the two in any number. The difference between (*a*) and (*b*) lay in whether the heavier lines executed last and on top of the others, crossed all the lines beneath them or only part of the lines beneath them. Since the frequency of (*a*) and (*b*) was similar at Green Lake and both were very unusual on other sites, the two were combined as Motif 7.

Motif 8 was defined by the blank triangular space formed by oblique incisions in opposite directions. Sometimes these opposing lines joined at the top, but this was infrequent.

Motif 9 was composed of horizontal lines. The number varied from one to eleven. On some vessels from the Oakfield and Kienuka Sites, however, there were motifs which by definition were included in Motif 9 and yet were also similar to Motif 13. These consisted of horizontal incised lines, usually a single one, with oval punctates or short cord-wrapped stick impressions above and perpendicular to the incisions. Since the decoration above was made by a different technique, by definition it was not part of the motif. The motif was classified as Motif 9. If the decoration above the horizontal lines had been made by the same technique as the horizontal lines, the whole would have been classified as Motif 13. This last motif occurred only with the technique of incising.

Motif 10 occurred only at the Green Lake Site. The impression of this decoration is that of a chevron, but each chevron was formed by two incisions with the lower executed last.

Motif 11, while rare in the Niagara Frontier, occurs on Neutral and Huron sites and so was distinguished (MacNeish, 1952: 36). It was, however, included as an atypical motif in the calculations. Motif 12 differed from Motif 6 in having vertical incisions above oblique incisions instead of oblique incisions above oblique incisions.

First, the motifs executed by incising only were compared for all sites. The frequencies of these motifs are shown in Table IV.

TABLE IV

FREQUENCY OF TYPICAL INCISED MOTIFS ON POTTERY VESSEL RIMS

Motif	Number of Vessels Represented						
	Site						
	Green Lake	Goodyear	Eaton	Buffam	Shelby	Kienuka	Oakfield
1	86	96	27	27	53	12	1
2	26	80	12	22	37	23	. .
3	25	39	8	20	13	6	. .
4	4	3	5	2	1	. .	. .
5	1	4	2	1	1	. .	. .
6	23	27	3	26	85	5	. .
7	15	1	. .	. .	. .	. .	. .
8	6	11	1	3	1	. .	. .
9	6	5	1	2	2	25	51
10	4	. .	. .	. .	. .	. .	. .
12	. .	. .	1	1	2	1	. .
13	. .	. .	. .	. .	. .	10	4
Total. .	196	266	60	104	195	82	56

When computing the coefficients of agreement for incised motifs, atypical motifs were omitted because my interest was in the conventional motifs which were used with the incised technique rather than in motifs which were unique or atypical. It is true, nevertheless, that some of the motifs called conventional or shared motifs occur with very low frequency and perhaps their repetition on two or more sites should be considered a chance repetition of a motif rather than a sharing of conventional pottery-decorating behavior in which traditional motifs persist. On the other hand, atypical decorations are also a measure of pottery-making behavior, showing the lack of conformity or lack of persistence of certain motifs. It is possible that some of these atypical motifs came from trade vessels from other areas, but except in a few instances it was impossible to determine this.

The arrangement of the sites which shows the least disorder is Green Lake, Eaton, Goodyear, Buffam, Shelby, Kienuka, and Oakfield, an arrangement which differs from the ideal by .3 per cent. This, however, is not one of the arrangements which might result from temporal differences. Some factor other than time must account for the high similarity between Green Lake and Eaton, which is responsible for their juxtaposition in this arrangement.

A second arrangement, Green Lake, Goodyear, Eaton, Buffam, Shelby, Kienuka, and Oakfield, differs from the desired order by .7 per cent. Since this is one of the arrangements of the hypothesis, this arrangement may be considered to represent the chronological order.

Comparisons were also made between the sites on the basis of combinations of motif and technique of decoration. Each category differed from all other categories by one attribute. For example, incised decorations of Motif 9 were distinguished from cord-wrapped stick impressed decorations of Motif 9. Similarly, cord-wrapped stick impressed decorations with Motif 9 were distinguished from those of the same technique which were decorated with Motif 13. In addition to the twelve categories of incised sherds shown by motif in Table IV, twelve new categories were added. Atypical decorations were included so that the comparisons were based on the total number of vessels from each site.

These twelve additional categories and their respective frequencies are shown in Table V.

The description of most of these categories is obvious. The third and fourth categories, "plain with punctates," and "motif of punctates," require explanation. The first includes those vessels which are undecorated except for a punctation at the base or top of the collar or a notch where the collar and lip join on the outside surface (Pl. III, Fig. 4). These punctates were not arranged to form a design or motif. On the other hand, in "motif of punctates," the punctations formed parallel rows or oblique lines or some other motif and occupied most of the rim or collar area (Pl. I, Fig. 5).

The next five categories in Table V represent a combination of a

TABLE V

FREQUENCY OF VESSELS BY TECHNIQUE OF DECORATION AND MOTIF

Technique and Motif	Number of Vessels Represented						
	Site						
	GL	G	E	B	S	K	O
Atypical incised	11	18	8	13	24	5	7
Undecorated	38	99	20	10	6	4	6
Plain with punctates	29	25	2	3	3	2	..
Motif of punctates	..	10	1	2	3	17	6
Cord-impressed, 1, 3	..	..	..	..	..	..	7
Cord-impressed, 9	..	..	..	..	..	..	7
Cord-impressed, 13	..	..	..	..	..	..	1
Cord-impressed, chevron	..	..	..	..	..	..	5
Cord-impressed, 8	..	..	..	..	..	..	1
Interrupted linear, 6	..	..	..	..	..	1	..
Interrupted linear, 9	..	..	..	..	..	11	17
Other techniques	8	2	2	1	1	9	16
Total	86	154	33	29	37	49	73

cord-wrapped stick impressed technique and a particular motif, as previously described. There are two categories of the interrupted linear technique, including push and pull and linear punch, with different motifs.

The best arrangement of the sites, Green Lake, Eaton, Goodyear, Buffam, Shelby, Kienuka, and Oakfield, differs from the desired arrangement by .1 per cent. This order, however, is not the chronological one since it differs from the arrangement of the hypothesis. The best arrangement which allows the inference of temporal order is Green Lake, Goodyear, Eaton, Buffam, Shelby, Kienuka, and Oakfield. This arrangement differs from the desired order by .3 per cent. Most of this disorder (.2 per cent) results from the position of the Eaton Site in this arrangement.

This attribute combination of technique and motif is the most useful of those considered for arranging the sites in an orderly fashion. The disorder produced by the comparisons of this attribute combination is lower than that for any other attribute class. This low disorder results from the fact that the number and amount of the individual coefficients which are out of order are low compared to those of other attributes. Second, the total of the differences between all pairs of coefficients is high. This high total indicates that the similarities and differences present a closer approximation to the desired order than do other attributes and are also subject to more variation in frequency, thus giving a more reliable arrangement. And yet it has been noted that the best arrangement of sites from comparisons of this attribute combination is not the best chronological arrangement for two of the sites. This is a strong argument for the unreliability of temporal sequences based on similarities and differences in a single attribute class or attribute combination. How much of this lack of reliability is peculiar to the data used here, i.e., the result of either small samples or high similarities between certain of the sites or a combination of these factors, is inascertainable.

Rim Profile. — There is some question as to whether the attribute class of rim profile properly belongs with the attribute classes of Group 1, those which show a consistent trend toward increasing or decreasing with respect to the frequency of the attribute and thus are useful for inferring chronology. The reasons for the hesitancy regarding the usefulness of the attribute class of rim profile will become clear as the discussion continues.

In recording the variations of rim profiles, two classes were recognized. The numerically smaller class consisted of profiles from vessels without collars. These were recorded by drawing the profile of each vessel rim. The second class, rim profiles of collared vessels, was recorded by means of description in terms of certain type profiles, each showing variation in one of the following attributes (Fig. 11):

1. Shape of exterior surface of the collar in radial section
2. Shape of interior surface of collar and neck in radial section
3. Relation of exterior surface of collar to interior surface of collar in radial section
4. Shape of the neck as it approaches the collar in radial section
5. Contour of the angle which exterior surface of collar forms with neck in radial section
6. Angle which exterior surface of collar forms with neck in radial section

Atypical profiles were recorded by sketching the individual forms.

It was clear from the difficulties encountered in recording rim profile and especially the large number of atypical forms that much more variation was present in rim profile than in other attribute classes. In order to reduce the unwieldy number of groupings used in recording the data, a reclassification of profiles from collared vessels was made by eliminating attribute 6 (above) from consideration. This resulted in a new set of classes, each differing by one attribute from every other class.

Attribute 1, the exterior surface of the collar as viewed in radial section, showed two variations, (*a*) straight or flat, and (*b*) concave. Attribute 2, the shape of the interior surface of the collar and neck, is that feature usually referred to as concave (channeled) or convex interior collar. On the interior of the vessel it is difficult to determine where the collar and neck join. For that reason the term "interior collar" refers to the interior area without concern for whether the channeling, straightness, or convexity was confined to the collar or continued onto the neck for a short distance.

Since this attribute showed continuous variation from very concave to very convex, the classification of certain intermediate forms was often uncertain. In order to classify these I placed a straight edge vertically along the interior surface. If there was a space near the center where the sherd surface did not touch the straight edge, it was considered concave. If, on the other hand, the straight edge did not touch both the top interior surface and the bottom interior surface because of some bulge in the center, it was considered convex. All others were straight. My procedure in classifying those collar interiors was consistent throughout, although another observer might not reach the same conclusions. In re-examining the sherds which MacNeish (1952) had previously typed, I found considerable lack of agreement in our handling of the sherds with respect to this attribute.

The relation of the shape of the exterior collar to the shape of the interior collar in radial section referred to three relationships. These relationships must be distinguished from attributes 1 and 2 which, for example, might be a straight exterior surface and a straight interior surface while the relationship between the two surfaces might show variation. These relationships occur: (1) the interior surfaces and the exterior surfaces are parallel, and there is no change in the thickness of the collar from top to bottom, (2) the surfaces are converging so that the collar at the top is thinner than at the bottom (in radial section), (3) the surfaces are diverging so that the collar at the top is thicker than at the bottom.

The shape of the neck as it approaches the collar in radial section was noted because some rim sherds had necks which curved outward sharply. This would presumably indicate vessels with short necks compared to those with longer necks as indicated from sherds showing little curvature. It is true that an estimation of this is scarcely accurate when it must depend on the size of the rim sherd as well as a guess as to what the curvature indicates about the form. Nevertheless, there were sherds which showed the neck nearly vertical in cross section while there were others in which the neck was beginning to curve outward sharply just a short distance below the collar. The frequency of vessels with outcurving necks must be regarded as representing a minimum and might have been more if larger sections of rim had been available. Profiles were classified as outcurving if they approximated the curvature shown in Figure 13, 2. All others were classified as straight (Fig. 13, 1).

The contour of the angle which the exterior surface of the collar forms with the neck in radial section may be described as either sharp or rounded. A sharp angle was formed when the bottom of the collar had a clearly defined edge resulting from the change in direction as the collar and neck joined. A rounded contour resulted when the change in direction was less abrupt and the collar rolled into the neck, without showing any obvious point at which the collar and neck joined.

The variations of these five attributes just described might combine to form seventy-two attribute combinations, each combination differing

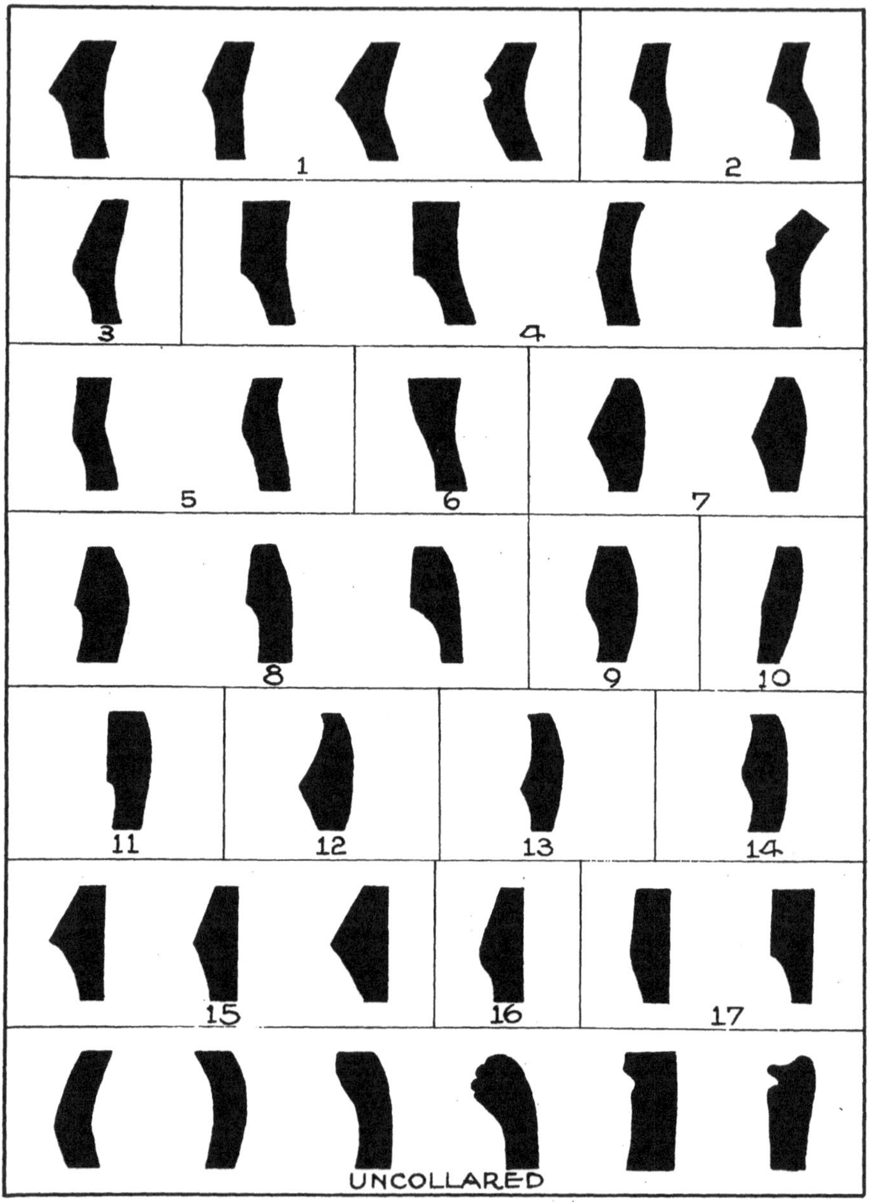

Fig. 13. Classes of Rim Profiles (Exterior to the Left).

from the others by a single attribute. Yet only seventeen of these combinations were represented by collared vessels from at least two sites. The following list describes each attribute combination which occurred at two or more sites. Figure 13 gives the appearance of the profile in radial section.

Class	Attribute 1	Attribute 2	Attribute 3	Attribute 4	Attribute 5
1.	straight	concave	converging	straight	sharp
2.	straight	concave	converging	outcurving	sharp
3.	straight	concave	converging	outcurving	rounded
4.	straight	concave	parallel	straight	sharp
5.	straight	concave	parallel	straight	rounded
6.	straight	concave	diverging	straight	rounded
7.	straight	convex	converging	straight	sharp
8.	straight	convex	converging	outcurving	sharp
9.	straight	convex	converging	outcurving	rounded
10.	straight	convex	parallel	straight	rounded
11.	straight	convex	parallel	outcurving	rounded
12.	concave	convex	converging	straight	sharp
13.	concave	convex	converging	outcurving	sharp
14.	concave	convex	converging	outcurving	round
15.	straight	straight	converging	straight	sharp
16.	straight	straight	converging	straight	rounded
17.	straight	straight	parallel	straight	sharp

The frequencies of vessels showing each of these attribute combinations of rim profile are shown in Table VI. All arrangements which were tried for the data on rim profile showed a comparatively high departure from the desired order. The closest approximation to the desired order was obtained by including the following data: Classes 1-5, 7, 8, 11, 13, 15, 17, and vessels without collars. The best arrangement of these data gave the following order of sites: Green Lake, Eaton, Buffam, Goodyear, Shelby, Kienuka, and Oakfield. This departs from the desired order by 2.3 per cent. This arrangement is not one of the possible arrangements in the hypothesis owing to the position of the Goodyear Site. Therefore, my conclusion is that some factor other than time must explain the similarity which places Goodyear in the center of the arrangement rather than toward the late end of the sequence as stated in the hypothesis.

Since this arrangement could not be considered as chronological, the next best arrangement was selected. This arrangement — Green Lake, Goodyear, Eaton, Buffam, Shelby, Kienuka, and Oakfield, agrees with one of the arrangements of the hypothesis. It departs from the desired order by 4.07 per cent.

Comparisons of the seven sites on the basis of similarities in profiles of collared vessels are also inconclusive. The best arrangement for the data of classes 1-5, 7, 8, 11, 13, 15, and 17, is Green Lake, Goodyear, Buffam, Eaton, Shelby, Kienuka, and Oakfield, with 4.9 per cent disorder. A second arrangement, Green Lake, Goodyear, Eaton, Buffam, Shelby, Kienuka, and Oakfield, has 7.9 per cent disorder.

TABLE VI

FREQUENCY OF CLASSES OF RIM PROFILES FOR COLLARED VESSELS

Class	Number of Vessels Represented						
	Site						
	Green Lake	Goodyear	Eaton	Buffam	Shelby	Kienuka	Oakfield
1	90	119	34	49	64	23	38
2	11	22	6	7	23	4	1
3	2	8	. .	. .	3	1	1
4	3	18	1	3	7	4	12
5	20	29	7	15	20	28	28
6	. .	4	. .	1	. .	. .	. .
7	34	18	6	8	13	6	. .
8	30	32	5	10	9	10	1
9	1	3	. .	. .	. .	2	. .
10	3	2	. .	. .	. .	. .	. .
11	2	6	1	. .	8	. .	1
12	. .	. .	2	. .	1	. .	. .
13	. .	2	. .	3	9	. .	. .
14	1	2	. .	. .	1	1	. .
15	25	27	3	5	10	7	1
16	1	6	. .	. .	. .	1	. .
17	12	23	3	3	2	5	. .
Total. .	235	321	68	104	170	92	83

In conclusion, the comparisons of rim profiles for all vessels as well as profiles of collared vessels only, allow inferences on the chronological order of four of the seven sites as follows: Green Lake, Shelby, Kienuka, Oakfield. The relative positions of Goodyear, Eaton, and Buffam, which fall in the sequence between Green Lake and Shelby, are not clear.

Summary and Conclusions

In the preceding discussion, five classes of ceramic attributes or attribute combinations have been selected for comparison because changes in their respective frequencies from site to site seemed orderly and explainable as changes through time. The attributes were: collared-uncollared, techniques of decoration, incised motifs, techniques of decoration and motifs, and rim profiles. The comparisons for each pair of sites were expressed by indices of likeness and these indices were ordered for each class following Robinson's method. The best arrangement for each class of attribute, or attribute combinations was selected and considered in the light of the hypothesis. In some cases the best arrangement of the data was not one of the chronological arrangements stated in the hypothesis. In these cases, indicated by an asterisk, in the arrangements below, the one selected was the best arrangement which was at the same time one of the alternative arrangements of the hypothesis. The percentage of disorder is indicated below each arrangement:

Collared-Uncollared	Decorative Technique	Incised Motif*	Technique and Motif*	Rim Profile*
GL	GL	GL	GL	GL
G	G	G	G	G
E	E	E	E	E
B	B	B	B	B
S	S	S	S	S
K	K	K	K	K
O	O	O	O	O
.3 per cent	1.4 per cent	.7 per cent	.3 per cent	4.1 per cent

Each of these five classes of attributes or attribute combinations showed that the best arrangement from which chronology could be inferred was Green Lake, Goodyear, Eaton, Buffam, Shelby, Kienuka, and Oakfield. In three cases, however, this site order was not the best order for the sites derived from comparisons of the data. Consistently, the relative positions of Green Lake, Shelby, Kienuka, and Oakfield remain the same. But there is some question about the relative positions of Goodyear, Eaton, and Buffam. Several arrangements in which the positions of Eaton and Buffam are reversed are nearly as satisfactory. Also the three best arrangements for incised motifs, technique and motif, and rim profile, show that the Eaton Site is closer to the Green Lake Site than is the Goodyear Site. In these same three arrangements the similarity between the Goodyear and Buffam Sites is higher than would be expected if the chronological order were that shown in the summary of the arrangements. The high similarity between Green Lake and Eaton on the one hand, and Goodyear and Buffam, on the other, cannot be explained as the result of temporal factors. But it is this high similarity which accounts for the difficulty in establishing the relative positions of Eaton and Buffam. For this reason it is necessary to examine more evidence bearing on the positions of these two sites.

Of those five attribute classes or attribute combinations in Group 1, the combination of decorative technique and motif seems most useful. Although this combination shows the same amount of disorder as the collared-uncollared arrangement, the site-to-site comparisons have less chance of being the result of sampling error. Rim profile, an attribute class often used in making pottery comparisons in the Northeast, was least useful of this group.

Attribute Classes of Group 2

In addition to the attributes and attribute combinations of Group 1, several other classes of attributes or attribute combinations show similarities or differences between some but not all of the sites under consideration. The Group 2 attribute classes serve to link some sites while separating them from the others. We can infer that those sites which are linked by the similarities of Group 2 attribute classes occupy a similar temporal position. Since the chronological relationship of most of the seven sites has already been inferred with more or less confidence from the attribute classes of Group 1, the similarities and differences among Group 2 attributes are now considered to be the result of chronological differences when they agree with the best arrangement arrived at so far. Thus the Group 2 attributes give additional evidence for the chronological sequence which was indicated by the attributes and attribute combinations of Group 1. In the case of the Eaton and the Buffam Street Sites, the relative position of which has remained dubious, certain attributes and attribute combinations of Group 2 were selected because they showed a difference between the sites which could be regarded as resulting from differences in time.

Castellations. — Several authors have pointed out the usefulness of the changes in castellation forms for inferring chronology (MacNeish, 1952: 31; Emerson, n.d.: 66-79). Castellations in the Niagara Frontier do not seem to have attained the popularity or the elaboration in form which they did in the Ontario area. For that reason the classification set up by Emerson on the basis of design and form changes was not suitable for the data from the Niagara Frontier. If larger samples were available, a more detailed classification, such as Emerson's, would be useful to accentuate the combined changes in form and decoration.

The classification here employed used only the shape of the rise above the vessel rim. These are pointed, rounded, squared, or bifurcated at the apex (Pl. IV). The squared castellations were frequently notched across the lip at the apex at one or two points (Pl. IV, Fig. 4). On some the notching seemed to cause the squared top. Others were squared by flattening the lip at the apex without the notches (Pl. IV, Fig. 5). Originally these two kinds of squared castellations were separated, but because of their low frequency it seemed useful to combine them. In no cases were the notches across the lip deep, and the class seemed clearly distinct from that of the bifurcated castellations.

Table VII shows the frequency and the percentage of each class of castellations.

The arrangement of the sites in this table is supported by the trends in popularity for pointed and squared castellations. Pointed castellations decreased in frequency from the time of the Oakfield Site, which according to the hypothesis is the earliest. The lowest frequency of pointed castellations at the Green Lake Site seems to be further support for its being the latest site in the sequence, as stated in the hypothesis. Except for the frequency at the Buffam Street Site, the decreasing popularity is consistent.

Squared castellations show in general an increase in popularity. They are absent at Kienuka and Oakfield. Beginning at the time of the

TABLE VII

FREQUENCY AND PERCENTAGES OF CLASSES OF CASTELLATIONS

Class	Number of Vessels Represented													
	Green Lake		Goodyear		Eaton		Buffam		Shelby		Kienuka		Oakfield	
	N	%	N	%	N	%	N	%	N	%	N	%	N	%
Pointed . . .	10	33	11	46	9	60	5	42	23	65	9	69	20	74
Rounded . . .	6	20	5	21	2	13	2	17	6	17	3	23	7	26
Squared . . .	12	40	8	33	4	27	4	33	5	15	. .	. .	. .	. .
Bifurcated .	2	7	. .	. .	. .	. .	1	8	1	3	1	8	. .	. .
Total	30		24		15		12		35		13		27	

Shelby Site, squared castellations reach their greatest popularity at the Green Lake Site. The popularity of rounded castellations fluctuates throughout the sequence. Bifurcated castellations are rare and sporadic.

The relative chronological positions of the Goodyear, Eaton, and Buffam Street Sites cannot be inferred with assurance from the frequencies of different classes of castellations. The position of Green Lake at one end of the sequence and Shelby, Kienuka, and Oakfield at the other seems to result from differences in the castellation frequencies which are due to differences in time.

Shape of Rim Interior on Collared Vessels. — MacNeish (1952: 34) has indicated a trend for an increased number of collars with convex interior surfaces on Huron sites as historic times are approached. In order to investigate this trend for the seven sites of the Niagara Frontier, the collared vessels from each site were separated into those with convex interiors and those with nonconvex (concave or straight) interiors. *Phi* coefficients were computed for each pair of sites and these were ordered. The resulting arrangement showed a pattern which might result from time differences in only two cases, Green Lake and Oakfield. The arrangement was not satisfactory for inferring the chronological order in general because of the similar frequencies of convex interiors at five sites. As a result of this, fourteen of the twenty-one comparisons by pairs of sites showed differences so slight that they could have occurred at least five times out of a hundred from sampling errors.

The Oakfield Site differed significantly from the others and had only 2 per cent convex rim interiors. Green Lake had the highest frequency of convex rim interiors, 31 per cent, but did not differ significantly at the 5 per cent level from several that were the most like it. The remaining sites had the following frequencies: Goodyear, 23 per cent; Eaton, 23 per cent; Buffam, 21 per cent; Shelby, 24 per cent; Kienuka, 21 per cent. Although the high frequency of convex interiors at Green Lake may result from sampling error, the difference is quite marked and can probably be ascribed to temporal factors. This attribute gives further support for the position of Green Lake at the late end and Oakfield at the early end of the sequence.

Neck Decoration. — Between the bottom of the collar and the shoulder, decoration sometimes occurred. Not included here were decorations at the shoulder itself or oval punctations in a single encircling row at the base of the collar. In some cases where the bottom of the collar was not sharply defined or where the vessels lacked a collar, the distinction between rim decoration and neck decoration was arbitrarily but consistently made on the following basis. A single horizontal row of oval or circular punctations very close to the base of the collar or on the rim was not considered neck decoration (Pl. III, Fig. 6). Two or more horizontal rows placed below the row on the rim of collarless vessels were considered neck decoration (Pl. I, Fig. 2). Incised lines or long punctations which might partially extend onto the collar area from the neck area were considered neck decoration.

Much of the neck decoration at the Oakfield and Kienuka Sites seemed to be a repetition of the decoration on the collar and rim and is, therefore, quite different from that at Shelby and Green Lake (compare Pl. III, Fig. 1 and 3). At Shelby and Green Lake the lines forming the neck decorations stopped at the bottom of the collar, and the collar had a different motif of incised lines in complicated designs. At the other three sites neck decoration is either completely or nearly absent.

At Oakfield the predominant class of neck decoration consists of an encircling row or several rows of vertical, oblique, or chevron designs formed by a variety of techniques (Pl. I, Fig. 2). These may start immediately below the collar or one quarter to one-half inch below. If there are several rows, they extend onto the neck for a distance, and the rows may be separated from one another by a short space. Forty-six per cent of the vessels at Oakfield are decorated in this fashion. Forty-seven per cent of these have the decorations formed by incision. One-fifth were formed by oval or rectangular punctations; one-sixth, by cord-wrapped stick impressions, and one-tenth, by dentate stamp impressions.

Another class of neck decoration occurs at Oakfield (Pl. I, Fig. 5). Six vessels have plats running obliquely down the neck from the collar. These are formed by rectangular or oval punctations, "fingernail" marks, or cord-wrapped stick impressions.

At Kienuka the encircling horizontal rows decreased in popularity to 34 per cent. The techniques by which these were made also changed. Half are made by incisions, 41 per cent by oval or rectangular punctations (Pl. I, Fig. 4), and only one may be cord-wrapped stick impressed but is very indistinct. The plat on the neck occurs on only one vessel where it is formed by an interrupted linear technique.

Neck decorations at the Shelby Site show considerable variation. Only two classes of these are similar to those from other sites. Two vessels have encircling oval punctates and argue for continuity from Oakfield and Kienuka. The other class, consisting of four vessels, has elaborate neck decoration of incised lines which begins immediately below the collar. Although it is impossible from the size of the sherds to determine the extent or motif of this decoration, it probably is similar to that on certain vessels from Green Lake.

On thirteen vessels from Green Lake, incised neck decoration is present. On one large section of a vessel incised lines extend from the bottom of the collar to the shoulder in opposed triangular areas (Pl. III, Fig. 3). Several other vessels may have been similar but are incomplete. They resemble somewhat the Huron type, Black Necked, but lack the neatness and closeness of incision pictured by MacNeish (1952: 36, 121). The presence of this type is not a time marker in the Huron sequence. The absence of neck decoration on vessels at Buffam, Eaton, and Goodyear raises the question of whether the vessels with elaborate neck decoration at Shelby and Green Lake are trade vessels.

The type and frequency of neck decorations at Oakfield and Kienuka link these sites. The similarity probably results from temporal factors. The absence of this type from later sites is further evidence that this is a temporal difference. The presence of neck decoration at Green Lake and Shelby is not useful as a time indicator.

Shoulder Decoration and Form. — Body sherds from all seven sites have oval punctations at the shoulder. It is likely that the frequency of this attribute differs from site to site, but data on the frequency are not available.

Vessel shoulders at the Green Lake Site are distinctive, both in form and decoration (Pl. III, Fig. 3). Several vessels occur with sharp shoulders. It is not clear whether these were locally made or were imported. Regardless of which was the case, their presence is important for they occur on no other known site in the area. This shoulder form is similar to the "carinated or ridged" shoulder of Ontario, but lacks the ridge (Emerson, n.d.: 85). Kidd (1949: 170) found carinated shoulders at Orr Lake, a historic Huron Site. At least one vessel from the Orr Lake Site which I examined in the collections of the Royal Ontario Provincial Museum has a shoulder like those from the Green Lake Site.

Complex shoulder decoration sets off the Green Lake Site from the other six considered. Not included here is a single row of punctations at the shoulder, a frequent feature on all the sites. The more complex decoration seems to be popular at Green Lake since 139 decorated sherds occur which are from either shoulders or necks. A few of these join to show several complicated patterns of opposed incised triangles at the shoulder. At least two vessels have horizontal incised lines at the shoulder while the rest were incised but too fragmentary to determine the pattern.

In Ontario, complex shoulder decoration occurs with a high frequency as a late feature, especially at Sidey McKay, a very early contact site (Emerson, n.d.: 87; MacNeish, 1952: 29). At the historic Huron Orr Lake Site, 30 per cent of the shoulders have complex decorations (Kidd, 1949: 175).

The presence of sharp shoulders and complicated shoulder designs suggests influence or trade with Ontario Iroquois. Although neither of these attributes is restricted to early historic times, there is further evidence which supports the conclusion that the similarities to Ontario pottery noted especially at Green Lake existed on the early historic time level.

Decorative Motifs. — Several decorative motifs occur at the Green Lake Site which suggest connections with Ontario Iroquois sites. The occurrence of Motif 10 only at Green Lake is one of these; the high frequency of Motif 7 at Green Lake is another. Three atypical (for the Niagara Frontier) designs represented by a single vessel each at Green Lake also have similarities in Ontario. Motif 7 and two of the atypical motifs fit the description of Warminster Crossed, which attains its highest frequency on historic Huron sites (MacNeish, 1952: 32). The third atypical motif occurs on the contact Benson Site (Emerson, n.d.: 228). Motif 10 is similar but not identical to motifs included in Sidey Notched, a type dominant in historic times (MacNeish, 1952: 33).

The presence of these motifs, along with the sharp shoulder and complex shoulder decoration, increases the differences between the Green Lake Site and the others in the Niagara Frontier. The presence of the new motifs is probably due to increased intercourse between groups during the early historic period. On the other hand, the appearance of these several attributes together and for the first time at the Green Lake Site may require additional explanation. The presence and general dominance of these features on early historic sites in Ontario strengthens the position of the Green Lake Site as latest in the sequence.

Surface Treatment of Body Sherds. — This attribute was of little use in the current study because data on the frequency of various treatments were not available for all sites. Body sherds with grooved paddle markings were found on all seven sites, but they occur in such small numbers that I suspect statistical treatment would be meaningless. Check-stamped sherds occur sporadically, but again seem to be strays. The change in the frequency of cord-marked body sherds is probably an important time indicator, but clear evidence of this is lacking. Cord-marked sherds are present on all sites except the Green Lake Site. The changing popularity of cord-marked body treatment from site to site seems to require two explanations: (1) a decrease in cord-marked bodies made locally as the popularity of smooth bodies increases, and (2) the presence of cord-marked bodies from non-Iroquois imported vessels or vessels made locally by women who were following a non-Iroquois pottery-making tradition.

The first, the decrease in cord-marked bodies, is part of a trend which MacNeish (1952: 82) noted as having begun in pre-Iroquoian times and which resulted in the disappearance of cord-marked bodies on vessels in Iroquois ceramics. Cord-marked bodies which are related to this trend occur on sites that are transitional to Iroquois and then cease to be a part of the Iroquois pottery-making tradition.

Yet cord-marked body sherds are found in small numbers on many Iroquois sites. If it were possible to study the spatial variation in the frequencies of cord-marked bodies from Iroquois sites of the same time level, the distribution would probably show that sites in the heart of the Iroquois area have lower frequencies of cord-marked bodies than do contemporary Iroquois sites from the fringes of the Iroquois area. This statement can be supported by noting the numerous cord-marked body sherds from the Ripley Site, an early historic Iroquois site on the border of the Iroquois homeland in southwestern New York. While no frequency can be stated for the number of cord-marked bodies at the Ripley Site, 16 per cent of the rim sherds were of a type (Ripley Corded) which has a cord-marked surface treatment (MacNeish, 1952: 24). This high frequency of cord-marking at Ripley is in sharp contrast with that at the contemporary Green Lake Site (from which it is about 60 miles distant) where no cord-marked body sherds occur. The higher frequency of cord-marking at Ripley seems to result from outside influences rather than from temporal differences. These outside influences may have taken the form of importation of cord-marked vessels or local manufacture by women who were following a non-Iroquois pottery-making tradition. In any event the high frequency at Ripley is probably unrelated to the trend toward body-smoothing.

The Oakfield Site certainly has the highest frequency of cord-marked bodies, but the actual proportion cannot be estimated reliably. On one small random sample of 175 body sherds, two-thirds were smooth, one-third were cord-marked. In another sample, which was selected so that it did not represent all the body sherds from a given excavation area, there were 100 smooth body sherds to 260 roughened bodies, most of which were cord-marked. These figures serve to indicate that cord-marked bodies were frequent at Oakfield.

For the Kienuka Site there are no figures on the proportion of cord-marked to smooth bodies. My impression is that smoothed bodies were in the majority, but there are more cord-marked sherds than at succeeding sites. One fabric-impressed body sherd was noted. At Shelby only two cord-marked sherds were noted among 800 body sherds. At the Buffam Street Site, about 2 per cent of the body sherds were cord-marked in a count of 500 sherds. In neither case am I certain that the sample represented all collected from a given area. At the Goodyear Site, in a sample of about 5,000 sherds, there was 1½ per cent of cord-marked body sherds. About 3,000 sherds from Green Lake showed no cord-marking.

A comparison of the several classes of surface treatment of body sherds from pottery vessels at the seven sites was of limited use for making chronological inferences because the data were not available to make precise statements. The frequencies of grooved-paddle and check-stamped body treatment are not part of any trends which have been recognized for Iroquois ceramics. Changes in the popularity of cord-marked bodies are part of a trend toward body smoothing which could not be shown from the data used here. A relatively high proportion of cord-marked bodies from the Oakfield Site is further evidence for its position early in the Niagara Frontier Iroquois sequence. The frequency of cord-marked bodies at Kienuka is unknown. The low frequencies of this same treatment at the remainder of the sites contrasted with that at Oakfield but allowed no conclusions about the temporal relationships of the Shelby, Buffam, Eaton, Goodyear, and Green Lake Sites.

Additional Rim Decoration. — Punctations, notches, and gashes, either above or below the main motif, or on otherwise undecorated collars, occur at all the sites (Pl. III, Figs. 4, 5, and 6). While the frequency of a particular kind of additional rim decoration in a specific location on the rim shows variation from site to site, no trends are evident throughout the series of sites. For this reason, additional rim decoration was included among the attribute classes of Group 2.

Notches at the junction of the lip and collar on otherwise undecorated vessel rims set off Green Lake and Goodyear from the other sites. Similarly placed notches on decorated vessel rims mark numerous vessels at the Shelby Site, but at the intervening sites of Eaton and Buffam there is a very low frequency of these notches. Thus the frequency of notches at the junction of the lip and collar does not offer any additional information on the chronological positions of the seven sites.

One specific form of decoration and its location on the rim appears to be useful for conclusions on the temporal relationships of some of the sites. A comparatively high frequency of punctations at the bottom of the rim links the Buffam and Shelby Sites more closely to each other than to the other sites (Pl. III, Fig. 6). These punctations, either oval or round, may be on the bottom of the collar at the junction of the collar and neck, or immediately below the collar. Twenty-six per cent of the vessels from Buffam and 42 per cent of those from Shelby show punctations in these positions. The frequencies at Kienuka (14 per cent), and at Oakfield and Eaton (15 per cent each) contrast with the high frequencies at Shelby and Buffam and negligible frequencies at Goodyear and Green Lake. If we accept the positions of Oakfield, Kienuka, and Shelby as established in that order, then there is evidence of a trend for the increase in punctations near the base of the collar which reaches a peak at Shelby, decreases at Buffam, and again at Eaton, and thereafter is very infrequent. The addition of punctations near the base of the collar is one of the few attributes in which the Eaton, Buffam, and Shelby Sites show differences with a low probability (less than 6 per cent) of being due to chance. Therefore, I conclude that on the basis of differences in this attribute, the Buffam Street Site is intermediate chronologically between the Eaton and Shelby Sites.

Specific Features of Castellations. — An examination of the differences among the castellations found on pottery vessels from the seven sites shows that there are frequently two specific attributes which occur singly or together on the castellations from Buffam Street and Shelby and which are rare or absent on castellations from the remaining sites. The first of these attributes consists of a vertical row of oval punctations, each aligned with its long axis perpendicular to the row (Pl. IV, Fig. 1). The row extends from the top of the exterior surface of the castellation to the bottom of the collar which is wide and lacks a heavy projection of either the collar or the castellation. There is no indication that the mouth form is other than round. The frequency of these oval punctations on this castellation form is higher at Shelby than at Buffam Street, although at both sites they are much more frequent than elsewhere in the Niagara Frontier. While oval punctations occur with castellations on the other sites, the punctations are usually beneath a heavy, overhanging collar and a thickened castellation.

Even more specific than the oval punctations in a vertical row are the ridges on which these punctations sometimes occur (Pl. IV, Fig. 1). The ridges, one of which was clearly an applique, were formed by a strip of clay about a quarter to a half inch wide. The strips were carefully welded to the vessel with no seams showing, and they extended from the peak of the castellation to the bottom of the collar. The oval punctations were arranged along these strips just as they were when the strips were absent. This combination of ridge and punctations on the ridge occurs also on vessels from the Reed Fort, Richmond Mills, Ontario County, New York (Parker, 1922: 182-207. Specimens in the Rochester Museum Collections). Here the collars are considerably higher (MacNeish, 1952: 51). These ridges occur on no other site in the sequence of the Niagara Frontier and are, therefore, important evidence of similarities between Buffam Street and Shelby.

These similarities at the Shelby and Buffam Street Sites in oval punctations placed in a vertical row on collars beneath castellations and often placed on a raised strip of clay as described above allow the inference that these two sites are more closely related temporally to each other than to the remainder of the sites on the basis of these attributes. These similarities are evidence for placing the Buffam Street Site earlier than the Eaton Site since the former is more like the Shelby Site whose position has been found to be earlier than either.

Width of Collar. — This attribute was recorded in measurement classes with intervals of one-fourth inch. Although there were differences in the distribution of the frequencies in these various classes at each site, there seemed to be no pattern or trend which could be interpreted to be the result of temporal changes. The vast majority of collars are under one inch. The frequencies of collars over one inch fall into two groups. The Green Lake, Goodyear, and Eaton Sites show a range of 5 to 8 per cent of the vessel collars over one inch, and the other four sites show a range of 12 to 18 per cent over one inch. However, the difference in this attribute between the Buffam Street Site and the Eaton Site, 5 per cent, could occur by chance nearly twenty-five times out of a hundred. Shelby has the highest frequency of wide collars. Perhaps width of the band of rim decoration would be a more accurate description since some fragmentary sherds were incomplete rims, and the width used was the minimum decorated area which was present. Eighteen per cent of the Shelby vessels have a decorated area with a width greater than one inch. There may be a tendency for narrower collars at Green Lake, Goodyear, and Eaton, but this needs further investigation from larger samples. If this tendency is validated, it will be further evidence that the Eaton Site is later than the Buffam Street Site.

Summary and Conclusions. — As a result of the consideration of the attributes of Group 1, those which allowed chronological inferences about the position of each site, the conclusion was reached that the probable chronological order from late to early was Green Lake, Goodyear, Eaton (?), Buffam Street (?), Shelby, Kienuka, and Oakfield. Now after considering other attribute classes which are useful for inferring the chronological position of certain sites in the sequence (Group 2), it is necessary to see how these agree with the former conclusion. Several additional attributes bear out the differences between Green Lake and the remainder of the sites and thus confirm the position of Green Lake as the latest in the sequence. They are: lowest frequency of pointed castellations and highest frequency of squared castellations, highest frequency of convex interiors of the collar profile, sharp shoulders, complex shoulder decoration, and several new decorative motifs.

Two attributes strengthen the conclusion that the Eaton Site is later than Buffam because of similarities between Buffam and Shelby. These attributes are: high frequency of punctations at the bottom of the rim and the presence of raised vertical strips and punctations beneath the castellations. A third attribute, that of slightly wider collars at Buffam compared to Eaton, has been considered worth further investigation from larger samples. If it can be shown that there is a tendency for wider collars at Buffam, these wider collars will link Buffam with Shelby and give further evidence for its position earlier than Eaton. Furthermore, the frequency of undecorated vessel rims, discussed in the attributes of Group 1, links Eaton more closely with Goodyear and Buffam with Shelby.

The position of the Kienuka and Oakfield Sites as early in the sequence is supported by a particular kind of neck decoration. The presence of plats on the necks of several Oakfield vessels in dentate and cord-wrapped stick impressed techniques point to the earliest position for the Oakfield Site since this attribute had high popularity in the preceding Owasco culture. The high frequency of cord-marked body sherds at the Oakfield Site also indicates the temporal priority of Oakfield.

This discussion of Group 2 classes of attributes does not include all the attributes which may be useful for establishing the chronological position of certain sites. It does include, of those attributes which I observed, all which show considerable differences between the Goodyear, Eaton, and Buffam Street Sites, still the weakest part of the sequence.

Attributes of Group 3

The attributes and attribute combinations of this group did not prove useful for establishing the chronological order of the sites under consideration. While numerous attributes might have been included, only three that have been frequently used in similar pottery studies are presented here. They are tempering material, combinations of rim decorative motif and rim profile, and previously defined pottery types.

The tempering material used in nearly all pottery vessels from Niagara Frontier Iroquois sites is grit. When shell tempering occurs, it is of very low frequency, representing probably one or two vessels. It is clear that changes in the kind of tempering material are of no use for making chronological inferences about these data.

Comparisons of the frequencies of the attribute combinations of rim motifs with rim profiles did not produce an orderly arrangement of the sites in terms of the hypothesis. The best arrangement for the twelve combinations with the highest frequencies produced the order Green Lake, Eaton, Buffam, Goodyear, Shelby, Kienuka, and Oakfield. The number of disorders and especially the size of these disorders suggested that inferences about time differences from this arrangement would be unreliable.

The reason for the lack of usefulness of this attribute combination lies in the large number of categories and the low frequency of most of them. For example, a selection of twenty-one attribute combinations of motif and rim profile accounted for all combinations which occurred on at least five of the seven sites. An examination of the attribute combinations which did not occur on at least five sites showed that no combination omitted had a frequency of ten or more at any single site. Yet these twenty-one combinations described a maximum of 59 per cent of the vessels at Eaton and a minimum of 25 per cent at Oakfield. In order to have taken into account most of the vessels from the sites an unwieldy number of combinations would have been required, for it seems that most of the motifs were combined with most of the rim profiles. For example with Motif 1, twelve different rim profiles occurred. When the number of combinations which are selected classify such a small part of the vessels from each site, the frequency of each combination is low, and the probability of differences resulting from sampling error is greater. It seems likely that this may be the major reason why an orderly arrangement does not result from these data.

Finally, there are the pottery types which have been defined for the area (MacNeish, 1952). I did not find that the similarities and differences among the types gave an orderly arrangement from which chronology could be inferred. Comparisons of type frequencies did indicate that Kienuka and Oakfield were earliest in the sequence. These same comparisons did not convincingly indicate the position of the other sites. Some of this uncertainty may result from my way of classifying the pottery into the defined types. Since the type categories were not mutually exclusive, it was often uncertain which of several types should have first consideration when classifying a particular vessel. Another difficulty was how strictly to observe the geographical limitations defined in the type. If no type defined for the area described the vessel and a type from a nearby area did, I used the foreign type. My use of this classification does not imply, however, that I think that these were foreign vessels. Figure 14 shows the percentage of the various pottery types from each site. All types are described by MacNeish (1952).

Summary and Conclusions. — An examination of three attribute classes of Group 3 did not offer any new evidence for systematic differences among the sites which allowed inferences about the temporal relationships among them. My conclusion about the chronological order of the seven sites as inferred from comparisons of ceramic attributes of Group 1 and Group 2 considered in the light of the hypothesis was that the order from late to early is: Green Lake, Goodyear, Eaton, Buffam, Shelby, Kienuka, and Oakfield. The evidence for the position of Eaton and Buffam is weak and alternate arrangements should be kept in mind in which Eaton precedes Buffam. Still a third logical possibility which could not receive substantiation through the method of analysis employed here is that the Eaton and Buffam Street Sites are contemporary settlements.

If the above arrangement of sites is the result of chronological differences, then the relative frequencies of the ceramic attributes should show systematic changes from site to site when arranged in chronological order. Ideally, the changes in the popularity of the various manifestations of each attribute will describe a lenticular shape if the changes are solely the result of chronological factors. The relative frequencies of the ceramic attributes of Group 1 are shown in Figure 14. The data used to compute the percentages are those of Tables II - VI. The percentages between each pair of solid vertical lines in Figure 14 total 100 per cent, where the total equals the number of vessels considered for that attribute. Column 1 is an exception since frequency changes in collared vessels are not shown because collared and uncollared vessels were the only manifestations of this attribute, hence together they equal 100 per cent.

Many of the columns in Figure 14 show the expected lenticular shape of change through time. Uncollared vessels, column 1, decrease through time. For the second attribute, techniques of decoration, the cord-wrapped stick impressed and interrupted-linear techniques, columns 2 and 3, decrease, while incising, column 4, increases and decreases. The changes in incised motifs are somewhat more irregular,

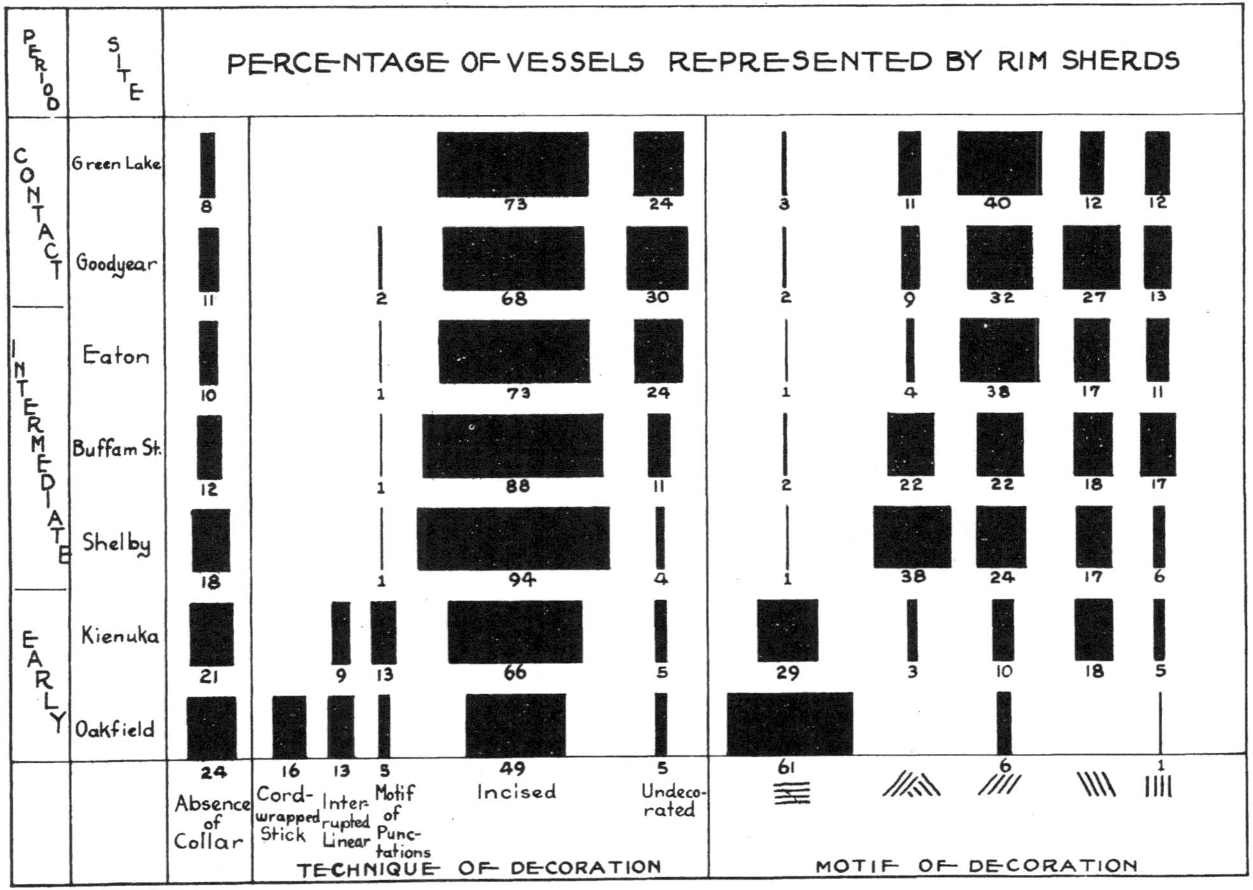

Fig. 14. Percentage of Pottery Types from Each Site.

showing graphically that with respect to certain incised motifs the Eaton Site is more similar to the Green Lake Site. Nevertheless, columns 7, 8, 9, 10, 11, 12, 15, and 18 show the expected pattern in general. Among the combinations of technique of decoration and motif, the same irregularity is manifest. Yet none of the columns diverges greatly from a lenticular shape. The manifestations of rim profile show, in general, slight and unpatterned change through time. Rim profile 5, column 47, demonstrates most clearly of this group a systematic change, in this case a decrease through time.

The data on ceramic attributes which were used to arrange the seven sites in chronological order by comparisons of similarities and differences in the frequencies of these attributes have been presented graphically according to the results of that arrangement. The resultant pattern is in most cases the lenticular one which systematic changes in the popularity of attributes manifest when the changes can be attributed to temporal factors. The evidence of Figure 14 supports the chronological order of the sites which was inferred from comparisons of the similarities and differences in the frequencies of ceramic attributes.

Pipes

Both ceramic and stone pipes have generally proved useful for pointing out the chronological relationships of Iroquois sites. Thus a seriation of sites based on a study of changes in the popularity of pipe styles should provide independent evidence for inferences on the temporal relationships of sites.

In the present study, however, a seriation of the 7 sites based on comparisons of pipe types from site to site appeared to be of questionable reliability. First, the sample of pipes and pipe fragments was small. A total of only 125 specimens was available for study from the seven sites. The smallest sample from a single site was 12 specimens from Oakfield; the largest sample was 24 from Eaton. Comparisons based on the frequency of different pipe styles would have shown a high probability of being the result of sampling error. Second, many (43 per cent) of the specimens were too fragmentary to ascertain the form accurately. Therefore, the occurrence of types of pipes on each site in the Niagara Frontier was compared to the sequence of types which had been recognized elsewhere in Iroquois territory. If a particular type of pipe had been recognized as a time marker on certain Iroquois sites outside the Niagara Frontier, the presence of that same type on a Niagara Frontier Iroquois site was regarded as evidence for assigning that site to the same general time period which the type marked outside the Niagara Frontier.

Because comparisons were to be made between specimens from Niagara Frontier Iroquois sites and other Iroquois sites the classification of pipes from the local sites conformed as closely as possible to that used elsewhere in Iroquois pipe studies. Classification of Iroquois

TABLE VIII

THE RELATIVE FREQUENCY OF POTTERY TYPES AT SEVEN SITES

Pottery Type	Percentage of Total Vessels at Each Site						
	Green Lake	Goodyear	Eaton	Buffam	Shelby	Kienuka	Oakfield
Neutral-Wenro							
Lawson Opposed	6	3	2	15	18	2	..
Lawson Incised	20	31	36	41	28	11	..
Pound Necked	1	1	..	..	..	..	..
Ripley Triangular	2	3	1	..	..	..	..
Ontario Horizontal	1	1	1	1	..	15	30
Middleport Oblique	..	..	..	..	..	12	3
Ontario Oblique	..	..	..	..	..	1	1
Iroquois Linear	..	..	..	..	..	8	14
Erie							
Ripley Plain	5	6	11	4	1	1	2
Niagara Collared	8	18	10	2	2	2	3
Ripley Collared	1	1	..	1	1	..	..
Huron							
Huron Incised	29	18	20	24	31	18	1
Warminster Crossed	2	1	..	..	..	..	..
Sidney Notched	1	2	2	1	2	..	..
Seneca							
Dutch Hollow Notched	7	5	..	2	1	..	..
Uren Corded	..	..	..	..	..	..	16
Uren Dentate	..	..	..	..	..	1	1
Atypical	17	11	16	9	16	29	29

pipes have usually been based on a primary division by material, i.e., ceramic and stone. Since ceramic pipes are much more numerous and have a less restricted distribution in time, further classification of them has been useful. Several archaeologists have used the form and decoration of the pipe bowl as the basis for classification (Emerson, n.d.; Ridley, 1952; Wray, 1956). I have also used a classification based on these attributes wherever possible. Since many of the specimens used in this study were fragmentary, the form was often doubtful and was based on the judgment of the writer. In the summary (Table IX, p. 95) the number of specimens on which form was estimated is shown in parenthesis.

The classification of ceramic pipes by combinations of bowl form and decoration will be described first. The occurrence of these combinations on Niagara Frontier Iroquois sites and on other sites will be discussed, and inferences on the temporal position of the Niagara Frontier Iroquois sites will be made.

Each specimen of the twelve stone pipes will then be described and comparisons made with similar specimens from other sites in order to attempt chronological inferences about them.

Ceramic Pipe Bowl Forms

The form classes for ceramic pipe bowls were as follows: acorn, rimless trumpet, rimmed trumpet, square bowl, effigy, other, and atypical. Most of these terms are familiar to those working in Iroquois archaeology so I shall describe them very briefly. "Acorn" refers to a bowl form like an acorn cup (Ridley, 1952: 201). (See Pl. V, Fig. 1.) Here, this class includes some of the forms which Emerson (n.d.: 46, 59-61) has classified as "bulbous" and "apple bowl."

"Trumpet" forms can be divided into rimless and rimmed trumpet bowls. Rimless trumpet forms are those with a flaring top, resembling that of a trumpet with the further requirement that the exterior sides of the bowl join the lip without flattening or without a rim. (See Pl. V, Fig. 2.) These trumpet forms lack the extreme flare of Huron forms (Emerson, n.d.: 46) and grade into conical forms. Rimmed trumpet forms have the same flaring of the bowl, but are flattened where the exterior side of the bowl joins the lip, forming a rim. Some rimmed trumpet forms have a greatly accentuated and overhanging rim with the decoration often restricted to this rim (Pl. V, Fig. 3).

"Square forms" refer to the shape of the exterior surface of the mouth of the bowl including the collar if present, as viewed from above. This class (Pl. V, Fig. 4) includes the classic "Huron pipe," Emerson's "coronet trumpet," and two divergent square tops (Ridley, 1952: 201; Emerson, n.d.: 60).

"Other" refers to forms with either straight or conical bowls as viewed from the side. This category includes fragments which are large enough to allow the judgment that the specimens do not have any of the forms previously listed. The fragments, however, are too small to observe whether the bowl constricts near the stem or whether the sides remain parallel, an observation which is essential to separation into conical or straight bowl forms (Pl. V, Fig. 5). "Atypical" refers to forms which differ from the usual Iroquois forms mentioned above. The atypical forms will be further described.

Decoration on Ceramic Pipe Bowls

Three classes of decoration were distinguished: plain or undecorated, incised rings, and other decoration. Rings or encircling lines are a very common motif on Iroquois pipes (Pl. V, Fig. 1). The number of rings may vary considerably, but all are formed by tightly spaced medium-wide incisions. Other decorations include vertical, oblique, or chevron motifs, made by incising, as well as motifs of punctations.

Combinations of Form and Decoration on Ceramic Pipe Bowls

Acorn Ring Bowls. — This combination occurs only at the Green Lake and Goodyear Sites. On Seneca sites it is popular from 1600-1650 only; after this period ring bowls tend to become more barrel-shaped (Wray, 1956: 15-16).

If I am correct in equating Emerson's "bulbous ring" type with the acorn ring bowl, then the latter has a similar temporal distribution in Ontario (Emerson, n.d.: 59-61). There the "bulbous ring" type occurs on late contact and early historic sites. Sidey MacKay, an early contact site, has this form. Some of the forms which Emerson has characterized as apple bowls are very similar also. Examples from the contact Benson Site fit this category, but the apple bowls from earlier sites seem less bulging (Emerson, n.d.: 112, 132, 152, 174, 212). Ridley (1952: 201) has found the acorn ring bowl on historic Huron sites.

The appearance of acorn ring bowls in the Seneca country and in Ontario on contact and historic sites supports the late position of Green Lake and Goodyear, which are the only Niagara Frontier sites having this class.

The acorn-shaped bowl seldom occurs without incised rings. There are no specimens which show this form with another decoration in the Niagara Frontier. One undecorated acorn bowl found at the Green Lake Site is unique.

Plain Rimless Trumpet. — The rimless trumpet form occurs either without decoration or with decoration other than rings. The plain rimless trumpet is found at the Eaton and Buffam Street Sites with slightly different forms. In Ontario this combination of no decoration and trumpet shape is regarded by Emerson as most frequent in the Intermediate Period, where it is very popular at the Lawson and Roebuck Sites. The plain trumpet pipe does continue into contact times at Sidey MacKay (Emerson, n.d.: 52-53).

TABLE IX

FREQUENCY OF PIPE CLASSES AT SEVEN SITES

Form and Decoration Combination	Number of Specimens						
	Sites						
	Green Lake	Goodyear	Eaton	Buffam	Shelby	Kienuka	Oakfield
Ceramic Pipes							
Acorn ring bowl	7	4	. .	. .	. .	. .	. .
Undecorated acorn.	1	. .	. .	. .	. .	. .	. .
Plain rimless trumpet	. .	. .	1	1	. .	. .	. .
Decorated rimless trumpet . . .	1	1	1(1)	. .	. .	. .	. .
Plain rimmed trumpet	2(1)	. .	. .	. .	. .	. .	. .
Decorated rimmed trumpet . . .	2(1)	2	3(1)	3(2)	1	1(1)	. .
Square Bowl	1	. .	1	3	3	. .	. .
Effigy							
Human	. .	. .	. .	2	?	. .	. .
Animal	. .	. .	1	1	. .	. .	. .
Bird	. .	2	. .	. .	. .	. .	. .
Undecorated other	5(2)	4(3)	7(6)	2	. .	4(2)	8(8)
Ring bowl other.	1(1)	2(2)	1(1)	1(1)	4(4)	1(1)	. .
Decorated other	. .	2	2	. .	7(4)	7(7)	. .
Atypical	. .	2	. .	1	3	. .	4(4)
Stone Pipes	1	2	7	. .	1	1(1)	. .
Total	21	21	24	14	19	14	12

In the Niagara Frontier the absence of plain trumpet pipes at sites other than Buffam and Eaton may well be due to small samples. Nevertheless, the presence of the plain trumpet pipe on these two prehistoric Niagara Fontier Iroquois sites which seem to belong to the same general time period as that during which these pipe forms have their greatest popularity in Ontario suggests that their temporal distribution in the Niagara Frontier may be similar to that in Ontario.

Decorated Rimless Trumpet. — The decorated rimless trumpet occurs at Green Lake, Goodyear, and Eaton. Neither the incised decorations nor the form are distinctive, and they do not approach the elaborate decoration or extreme flare of Canadian forms. The presence of these forms on Niagara Frontier Iroquois sites does not allow chronological inferences.

Plain and Decorated Rimmed Trumpets. — Rimmed trumpet forms are much more common than the preceding category in the Niagara Frontier. Most are decorated; only two plain specimens occur in a total of fourteen pipes. Both of the undecorated specimens are from Green Lake. Decorated specimens invariably have short incisions or punctations on the rim, and occasionally they occur on the lip. Rimmed trumpets have been found at all sites except Oakfield, and some variety of form exists within the category. Slightly flaring-sided bowls with either vertical or insloping rims occur on some examples; others have a sharp flare at the juncture of the sides and rim (Pl. V, Fig. 3). One of the latter at Goodyear has a very narrow rim, but the sharp flaring produces a wide lip. Punctate decoration occurs on the lip and on the rim.

Emerson (n.d.) does not describe the rimmed trumpet form in his analysis of pipe types in Ontario. The rimmed trumpet form does occur in Ontario in the Lalonde of the Huron country. One pipe from the Buffam Street Site is identical in form to the Classic Lalonde trumpet (Ridley, 1952: 204), but is smaller. The trumpet pipe however, has wide temporal and spatial distribution, and this comparison need not imply contemporaniety. The form is common on Mohawk-Onondaga sites and present, but rarer, in the western part of the state according to Parker (1922: 148). It is well represented on Niagara Frontier sites. Forms like those in the Niagara Frontier occur also at Ripley and have a similar range of form (Parker, 1922: 297, Nos. 5, 6). A more detailed classification of trumpet pipes from an area with larger samples and more complete specimens might be useful for establishing chronological relationships throughout the Iroquois territory.

Square Bowl. — Square bowl pipes have been found at Shelby, Buffam, Eaton, and Green Lake. Their absence at Goodyear is probably not significant as their frequency is not great at any site. In Ontario, square bowls reach their peak of popularity in contact times, but are present throughout a large part of the sequence, beginning with the McKenzie

Site (Emerson, n.d.: 59, 230). Therefore, their presence is not useful as an indicator of time.

Effigy Forms. — Effigy forms representing both humans and animals occur in the Niagara Frontier Region. They are absent at Oakfield and Kienuka. A human head effigy form may occur at Shelby, for one was reported to me by Owen (personal communication). A second, said to be from Shelby, was on exhibit in the Buffalo Historical Society. Since the specimen was uncataloged, I am somewhat reluctant to accept it. One argument for its provenience at Shelby is its general similarity to two specimens from Buffam Street.

One of the two human effigy pipes from Buffam Street is known only from a photograph (Pl. V, Fig. 6). The other lacks the stem and part of the bowl. These pipes do not closely resemble forms I have seen from surrounding areas, but they are in the general pattern found at the Roebuck Site. Emerson (n.d.: 62) judged the Roebuck style of human effigy to be a marker for the Intermediate to Contact Period. This style is quite different from the pinched nose and blowing figures of historic times.

Fragments of a single animal effigy pipe were found at Eaton and at Buffam. Both examples appear to be very similar and have been called bear effigies. The interior pipe bowl is situated just back of the animal's ears so that the animal is part of the bowl rather than an appendage, as it is on Seneca and Ontario Sites. In Ontario the bear is an Intermediate to Contact Period marker, but because of the difference in form this placement may not be applicable to the Niagara Frontier (Emerson, n.d.: 50). A part of another pipe bowl, probably from Eaton, may be a snake effigy, but this identification, like the provenience, is uncertain.

Two bird effigies come from the Goodyear Site. Neither are familiar forms from other areas. On both specimens the bowl interior is part of the bird's body and the head forms the front of the bowl, away from the smoker. Again exact parallels are absent for comparison. No effigy pipes occur at the Green Lake Site.

Other Forms. — The class "other" contains forms that were either straight or slightly conical. Undecorated pipes with these forms are the most frequent. They occur on all sites except Shelby. Because of their high frequency, they are probably useful in distinguishing the sites of the Niagara Frontier from surrounding areas, but seem of no value at the present for pointing out chronological relationships.

Fragments of conical or straight forms with decoration are also frequent. These occur at Kienuka, Shelby, Eaton, and Goodyear. These are quite simply and carelessly decorated with punctations or short incisions near the top. No meaningful pattern of frequency was discernible within this group. Conical or straight ring bowl forms are present throughout the sequence, except at Oakfield. No specimen is complete, but the fragments indicate that the form is neither a trumpet nor an acorn ring bowl.

Atypical Forms. — Several distinctive forms are limited to a single site or a single specimen. One punctate-decorated collared pipe from the Goodyear Site resembles closely specimens from the Sidey MacKay site in Ontario. Emerson (n.d.: 59) did not find this form on prehistoric sites in Ontario, a circumstance consistent with the position of the Goodyear Site as a contact site.

At the Oakfield Site two unique pipes occur. Both are incomplete so that no judgment of the angle of stem and bowl is possible. One has a square bowl with incised chevrons. The second is decorated with very fine cord-wrapped stick impressions and probably had a globular body. Except for a few plain fragments of pipe bowl, the pipe complex at Oakfield shows no similarities in form or decoration to later sites in the area. This is further evidence for its early position.

Three fragmentary pipes from the Shelby Site are intermediate in form between the straight ring bowl and the acorn ring bowl. These probably had short bowls decorated by two or three rings. Below the bottom ring the bowl contracts sharply, giving the effect of a ringed collar. The fragments lack the bulge of the acorn forms and the height of the straight-sided ring bowls. Since these pipes are fragmentary, description of this type should await more complete specimens.

Stone Pipes

Stone pipes have been found on all sites except Oakfield and Buffam. The form at Kienuka is unique, however. It has a rectangular bowl decorated with punctations. The stone bowl from Shelby is too fragmentary to determine its form. The ten remaining forms from Eaton, Goodyear, and Green Lake are predominantly vasiform and barrel-shaped, and a general similarity of form marks these specimens.

The absence of stone forms at Buffam compared to the presence of seven vasiform and barrel-shaped specimens at the Eaton Site suggests a significant difference between these sites. A *chi square* test indicates that this difference would occur by chance about 2.5 times in a hundred. The interpretation of a genuine difference between Eaton and Buffam is supported further by the occurrence of stone pipes like the Eaton specimens on the Green Lake and Goodyear Sites, on the earliest contact Seneca Sites, and in late prehistoric and early historic sites in Western New York and Pennsylvania (Wray, 1956; Witthoft, Schoff and Wray, 1953: 94). This evidence clearly suggests that the Eaton Site is later than Buffam.

The single specimen from the Green Lake Site shows surprising similarity in form to the Warren Site and the Dutch Hollow Site examples (Witthoft, Schoff and Wray, 1953: 105, No. 4; Ritchie, 1954, 49, No. 3). Each of these three has decoration scratched on the surface.

The Warren Site has been dated at 1615-1630 and the Dutch Hollow Site from 1590 to 1615 (Wray and Schoff, 1953: 56; Ritchie, 1954: 70). This late dating would seem to strengthen the position of the Green Lake Site as the last in the Niagara Frontier sequence.

Summary

The pipes from the seven sites in the Niagara Frontier have been described by form and decoration. They have been compared to pipes of related types from Ontario and from Seneca sites, where their chronological position is better known. It has been assumed that their position in the Niagara Frontier is the same as in neighboring areas. The acorn ring bowl and stone pipes both indicate late positions for Green Lake and Goodyear. A specific stone bowl form at Green Lake and a collared clay form at Goodyear give similar indications. The presence of several stone pipes at Eaton and the complete absence at Buffam Street link the Eaton Site with Green Lake and Goodyear. On the other hand, plain unrimmed trumpet forms and bear (?) effigy forms at Eaton and Buffam distinguish them from the others. Human effigy pipes occur at Buffam and probably at Shelby. Oakfield shares only undecorated straight or conical forms with the other sites. Table IX contains a summary of the combinations and their frequencies at each site. The number in parenthesis indicate those which were so fragmentary that the bowl form is somewhat speculative.

The chronological positions of the sites as inferred from the pipe comparisons agree in general with the best temporal arrangement established from similarities and differences in ceramic attributes, although the exact position of particular sites is not as clear. For example, the pipe classes at Green Lake and Goodyear do not reliably show the relative position of these two. On the other hand, the pipe comparisons give important evidence on the relative positions of the Shelby, Buffam Street, and Eaton Sites. The best chronological arrangement, on the basis of pottery and pipe attributes and attribute combinations is as follows: Green Lake, Goodyear, Eaton, Buffam, Shelby, Kienuka, and Oakfield.

Projectile Points

Projectile points were investigated for their usefulness in ranking sites in temporal order because it seemed that they had been generally overlooked in most discussions of artifact changes through time in the Iroquois area. It is well known that the projectile points of the Owasco and similar cultures were broad triangles (Ritchie, 1944: 50), while those of the historic Iroquois were small isosceles triangles. Under the hypothesis that the size of projectile points in the Niagara Frontier might have undergone a systematic change from a broad triangle to a smaller triangle and that this change might reflect temporal differences,

TABLE X

AVERAGE LENGTH, WIDTH, AND STANDARD DEVIATIONS OF PROJECTILE POINTS

Site	Average Length (Inches)	Average Width (Inches)	Standard Deviation (Length)	Standard Deviation (Width)	Number
Green Lake . . .	1.21	.66	.23	.09	43
Goodyear	1.11	.63	.20	.08	96
Eaton.	1.20	.58	.18	.11	87
Buffam.	1.20	.70	.28	.17	72
Shelby	1.19	.64	.25	.10	28
Kienuka	1.22	.68	.23	.11	34
Oakfield	1.38	.95	.23	.20	22

the sizes of triangular points from the seven sites were compared. Those selected for measurement were triangular in form and two inches or less in length. This criterion of size eliminated several specimens which met the requirement of form but which seemed too large and heavy to serve as projectile points.

The average length and width were computed for each site. The total sample of 382 specimens ranged from 22 at Oakfield to 96 at Goodyear. The average lengths and widths were listed according to the best arrangement from previous considerations in the order: Green Lake, Goodyear, Eaton, Buffam, Shelby, Kienuka, and Oakfield. The differences between the average lengths and average widths for each pair of sites were compared in accordance with the hypothesis. The significance of the difference in the means was tested for certain pairs of sites, including all those sites which were adjacent in the listing. The data are given in Table X.

In average length, only two sites, Oakfield and Goodyear, show a marked difference from the others. Of these two, only the difference at Oakfield seems attributable to temporal factors in the light of the above hypothesis. This difference in average length between Oakfield and the other sites would occur in all cases less than five times out of one hundred due to chance, according to Student's t test. Except at Oakfield, the slight differences between the means and the high chance of this resulting from sampling error make changes in projectile point length of little value for inferring chronological order.

The average widths of projectile points show considerably more variation. Even though the differences between individual means are small, the standard deviations are very similar, except those at Buffam and Oakfield, and most of the differences are below the 5 per cent level of significance.

The probability that the differences in average width between pairs of sites are attributable to sampling error is:

Green Lake - Eaton	Less than 1 per cent
Green Lake - Oakfield	Less than 1 per cent
Goodyear - Eaton	Less than 1 per cent
Goodyear - Buffam	Less than 1 per cent
Goodyear - Kienuka	Less than 1 per cent
Goodyear - Oakfield	Less than 1 per cent
Eaton - Buffam	Less than 1 per cent
Eaton - Shelby	Less than 1 per cent
Eaton - Kienuka	Less than 1 per cent
Eaton - Oakfield	Less than 1 per cent
Buffam - Oakfield	Less than 1 per cent
Shelby - Oakfield	Less than 1 per cent
Kienuka - Oakfield	Less than 1 per cent
Green Lake - Buffam	2 per cent - 5 per cent
Green Lake - Goodyear	5 per cent - 10 per cent
Buffam - Shelby	5 per cent - 10 per cent
All others	More than 10 per cent

If the sites are arranged according to the order arrived at from the previous evidence, the changes in average width do not correspond to those suggested in the hypothesis about the temporal changes in projectile point size. To do so, the average widths would have to show a decrease from .95 inches at Oakfield to the smallest width at Green Lake. Still, a decreasing trend is evident through part of the sequence: Oakfield, .95; Kienuka, .68; Shelby, .64; Eaton, .58. This arrangement within the entire sequence might arise by chance about twelve times out of one hundred, according to Kendall's *tau* test. Average widths at Buffam, Goodyear, and Green Lake do not show a decrease. From this evidence it is not clear whether the changes in average width through time as seen at the sites support the hypothesis. It is worth further investigation when samples from more sites are available.

Perhaps the most important conclusion to be drawn from the ranking of sites by length and width of projectile points has to do with the difference between the projectile points at Oakfield and those at the other sites. Clearly the points there are larger and offer additional evidence for the position of Oakfield as earliest in the sequence. In the time interval between the Oakfield Site and the rest of the sequence, there was a decided reduction in size. By the time of the Kienuka Site, the length had become well fixed. The greatest change in average width had already taken place during the interval between Oakfield and Kienuka, but some patterned change may continue to the time represented by the Eaton Site.

The form of projectile points as described by combinations of the shape of the sides and the shape of the base did not show any orderly change. Perhaps these combinations would be useful in indicating the popularity of certain forms on certain sites. But comparisons of the differences between sites show no order which can be inferred to be the result of chronological differences. From the standpoint of projectile point size, Oakfield is set apart from all the other sites. Changes in length thereafter were not useful for my purposes. Changes in width, however, did occur, and they may indicate a trend toward a reduction although the evidence is not strong.

Summary of the Archaeological Evidence

The comparisons of projectile point sizes conclude the presentation of the evidence which bears on the chronological position of the seven Niagara Frontier Iroquois sites. Comparisons of the similarities and differences of selected attributes and attribute combinations have been made for each pair of sites in order to make inferences about the temporal relationships of the sites. Pottery attributes in general proved to be the most useful for these purposes. Certain classes of attributes or attribute combinations such as the presence of collars, motifs of decoration, techniques of decoration, and rim profiles were common to the pottery of all sites. The differences in various manifestations of these attribute classes were orderly and temporal changes seemed to be indicated. Although the ordering of the sites by these attribute classes considered independently did not give the same results in each case, the bulk of the evidence supported two alternate arrangements from the twelve presented in the hypothesis: Green Lake, Goodyear, *Eaton, Buffam*, Shelby, Kienuka, and Oakfield, or Green Lake, Goodyear, *Buffam, Eaton*, Shelby, Kienuka, and Oakfield. These two arrangements were then used as the only alternate arrangements in further investigations to determine which of them best represented the chronological order.

Additional classes of ceramic attributes were restricted in their distribution among the sites. Therefore, the following classes gave evidence in support of certain parts of the sequence: castellation forms, interior shape of collar profile, neck decoration, shoulder decoration and form, certain decorative motifs, surface treatment of body sherds, additional rim decoration, certain features of the castellations, and width of collar. These attribute classes supported the above arrangements throughout. Furthermore, two and possibly three indicated that the Buffam Street and Shelby Sites shared certain attributes which the others did not. An additional attribute class gave evidence that the Eaton Site was closer to Goodyear than the former was to Buffam Street. Therefore it seemed likely that the Eaton Site was later than the Buffam Street Site and the best arrangement was: Green Lake, Goodyear, Eaton, Buffam, Shelby, Kienuka, and Oakfield. This arrangement, however, resulted entirely from a consideration of ceramic attributes. It was necessary to see how this arrangement was supported or refuted by settlement pattern, pipes, and projectile points. Several features of the settlement pattern and burial practices in no way contradicted this arrangement. The presence of an earth bank linked Oakfield, Kienuka, Shelby, and Buffam Street. The presence of numerous grave goods and European trade materials at Green Lake and Goodyear pointed to historic positions for these sites.

The occurrence of pipe classes also supported the order of Green Lake, Goodyear, Eaton, Buffam, Shelby, Kienuka, and Oakfield. The evidence for this arrangement was adduced from comparisons with the Ontario and Seneca sequences, where much larger samples of pipes have been used to infer chronological differences. The differences in pipe classes were especially important in strengthening the evidence for the position of the Eaton Site as later than the Buffam Street Site.

Changes in the size of triangular projectile points gave some additional support to the preferred chronological arrangement of the sites. Points at the Oakfield Site were larger in both average length and width. Average length showed little temporal change other than this. A possible trend toward a decrease in average width was discernible from Oakfield through Kienuka and Shelby and again at Eaton. At the Buffam, Goodyear, and Green Lake Sites there was an increase in width which is more difficult to account for.

The total evidence considered supports the following ranking for the sites in the Niagara Frontier: Green Lake, Goodyear, Eaton, Buffam, Shelby, Kienuka, and Oakfield. It was assumed at the beginning of the study that differences between these sites were the result of chronological differences because the sites were located in a small, homogeneous geographical area. Therefore the above arrangement is the best chronological arrangement, from late to early, for the sites of the Niagara Frontier Region.

VIII

THE CULTURE HISTORY

Introduction

The sites of the Niagara Frontier have been arranged in chronological order from early to late with the result: Oakfield, Kienuka, Shelby, Buffam Street, Eaton, Goodyear, and Green Lake. This temporal succession will be referred to as the Niagara Frontier Iroquois sequence. This sequence in time will now be located in terms of an absolute chronology, and the changes which occurred in Iroquois material culture in the Niagara Frontier during the period covered by the data from these sites will be described. First, the chronological framework will be discussed, and the sites will be assigned to either the Early, Intermediate, or Historic Periods.

Chronological Framework

In establishing a chronological framework to examine culture continuity and change in the Niagara Frontier, the culture of each site may be considered as representative of the culture in this area for a particular segment from a temporal continuum. Each segment which is represented may be considered to have about the same time span. This in fact is not true, but since historic Iroquois villages moved every fifteen to twenty-five years, the problem of whether a given segment represented by a village occupied twenty-five years, more or less, is of no consequence in terms of the temporal span which we are considering (Wray and Schoff, 1953: 53).

One can assume, then, that the segments occupy the same interval of years in the continuum without serious error. These segments are not equally spaced along the continuum, however. There is no reliable procedure based on typology which will allow an assessment of the relative or absolute time intervals separating them. For example, one might suggest that the segments represented by Goodyear, Eaton, and Buffam are closely spaced because of the similarities of pottery. On the other hand, one might emphasize the differences in pipes or castellations, viewing these as more indicative of temporal differences than pottery decoration. There appears to be no satisfactory solution to this particular problem in terms of the existing data. Therefore, no absolute dates can be assigned to the sites of the seriation by inferences from the rate of culture change.

A future approach to the problem of dating sites stems from the fact that Iroquois villages generally followed an orderly pattern of movement for a distance of several miles along the course of a stream. It would be possible, for example, to investigate the number of villages intervening along the course of Buffalo Creek which might connect the Buffam Street Site with the Goodyear Site. Such a procedure would allow statements on the total number of villages included in the time span and more reliable estimates of the time involved, under the assumption that each village occupation represented the same interval of time.

Another approach to this same problem would be an estimate of the total time span occupied by the framework. One end is firmly based in the early Historic Period. The other end involves more speculation. MacNeish (1952: 86) has dated Transitional Iroquois from A.D. 1100 to 1350. A radiocarbon date (M-651, Crane and Griffin, 1959: 183) of 420 ± 150 years ago has been obtained from the Oakfield Site. It is difficult to assess the reliability of this single date. It is clear that if the true date lies within the range of one standard error, it must be close to the earlier end of the range, about 1400 A.D. This date has been discussed elsewhere (Pechuman, 1958; White, 1958). If it correctly dates one part of Transitional Iroquois, we must conclude that Transitional Iroquois lasted somewhat later than previously supposed. A span of four to five hundred years for the duration of Transitional Iroquois and Iroquois into the early Historic Period seems reasonable.

The handful of sites excavated for any limited geographical area covers a small part of this period. In the Niagara Frontier, the intervals between Oakfield and Kienuka and between Kienuka and Shelby are probably the longest since formal differences are more numerous in these instances. By the same reasoning, the interval between Goodyear and Green Lake is small. From comparisons with the Seneca sequence, I suggest that the dates for these two sites fall within the following spans: Goodyear, 1550-1600; Green Lake, 1575-1625 (White, 1958). I suggest no dates for the prehistoric sites.

Nevertheless, it is useful to assign the sites to chronological periods, even if these must be regarded as relative rather than absolute. The establishment of chronological periods allows more systematic generalizations about changes in certain aspects of material culture in the Niagara Frontier Region. Moreover, this kind of terminological distinction makes clear that there is a difference between the culture type and chronological periods, even if the latter are arrived at in this case through inferences from the former. Furthermore, these relative chronological periods should be regarded as a first step toward an absolute chronology. Once an absolute time framework is available, it can be extended without spatial limitations to serve as one basis for cultural comparisons. In the absence of chronological periods, the beginning and end of which can be defined as a specific point in time, a relative chronological framework can be useful for comparing the cultures from nearby areas. These periods can be delimited by selecting certain typological criteria as markers. It is necessary to assume that these typological markers were in existence contemporaneously throughout the areas to be compared. This is certainly an oversimplification, but until absolute dates are available, it is the best possible procedure.

Emerson has similarly established a chronological framework in Ontario by using Iroquois pipe types. He pointed out that certain types were markers for the Early, Intermediate, and Historic and Late Prehistoric Periods (Emerson, n.d.: 45), but he did not assign sites to these periods since he was interested in a different problem. For the Niagara Frontier data, comparisons of pipes between sites within the area and outside the area were limited in usefulness by the small samples and fragmentary nature of the specimens. It is likely that certain pipe types will prove to be the best time indicators as there seems to be marked similarity in forms and decoration as well as systematic changes in the popularity of the types throughout the Iroquois area. But present data are insufficient to be useful for chronological markers.

MacNeish (1952: 7, 87) has used aberrant sherds or trade sherds to set the sequences from the several tribal areas in relative chronological positions without defining chronological periods. I was unable to use this approach because the recognition of trade pottery made by neighboring groups is very difficult. Therefore, it seemed advisable to assign names to periods in order to generalize about culture changes in the Niagara Frontier sequence and in order to have a convenient framework to set up comparisons with sites from surrounding areas.

Three time periods are recognized, the Historic, Intermediate, and Early Periods. The marker for the Historic Period is the presence of European trade goods. In this period are those sites (often called Protohistoric or Contact) with European trade goods which probably were obtained by Indians in this area in some manner other than by direct contact with Europeans. Also there are sites from the time when historic documents indicate Europeans were in the area. Preceding the Historic Period is the Intermediate Period. Iroquois sites are assigned to the Intermediate Period on the basis of the absence of the artifacts which are markers for the Historic and Early Periods. The Early Period is characterized by certain features which are transitional to Iroquois culture. The time marker is the presence of pottery rim decoration made by cord-wrapped stick, interrupted linear, or dentate stamp techniques together with incised rim decoration.

The Historic Period corresponds to the Late Woodland V Period, the Intermediate to Late Woodland IV, and the Early to part of Late Woodland III (Ritchie, 1951: 132).

The periods, Historic, Intermediate, and Early, have been in use previously or have been implicit in the thinking about Iroquois development. A Late Prehistoric Period is also frequently used to include those sites directly ancestral to sites showing the earliest European trade goods. I was unable to find a typological marker to define the inception of a Late Prehistoric Period. The Intermediate Period probably includes by far the greatest number of sites and consequently the longest period of time. It should be subdivided when the appropriate marker can be found.

Site Classification

It remains to relate the sites of the Niagara Frontier sequence terminologically to the various classifications to which they might pertain. This requires an examination of the classifications currently in use. These reflect two major approaches to Iroquois archaeology, the Midwestern Taxonomic Method and the direct historical approach. Each of the three archaeologists whose classifications are in use in the Iroquois area have given consideration to both of these approaches.

In 1944, Ritchie (1944: 5), using the Midwestern Taxonomic Method, classified the late prehistoric and historic cultures of New York into the Iroquois Aspect, Upper Phase, Mississippi Pattern, and the Owasco Aspect, Northeastern Phase, Woodland Pattern, and listed the distinguishing traits of the Owasco (341-33). Later it was recognized that the Iroquois Aspect was not part of the Mississippi Pattern (Ritchie, 1951: 132; MacNeish, 1952: 88). Under this system sites were classified on the basis of similarities and differences of traits without respect to the ethnic identity of the inhabitants. Theoretically, a site inhabited by Algonquin-speaking people would be classified as part of the Iroquois Aspect if the required per cent of its traits was diagnostic of the Iroquois Aspect. The identification of a site or focus with an ethnic group was a separate problem. Under this system the name "Iroquois Aspect" was an unfortunate choice, since sites of Algonquin-speaking as well as Iroquoian-speaking people might be included under it.

In 1952, Ritchie described five sites in Eastern New York which he has called the Chance Horizon. He has identified this group of sites as an early stage of Mohawk. At the same time he has indicated the advisability of postponing the definition of a focus or foci composed of this group because of the lack of data in the general area (Ritchie, 1952: 5). It is usual to delay inferences about the tribal identification of sites until a descriptive unit based on typological similarities has been formed unless there is independent evidence for the identity of the inhabitants. Even when a focus of sites has been defined, it cannot be assumed that any single factor such as tribal identity will account for all the similarities common to the group, or that the same set of factors will explain the similarities found among all pairs of the group. Ritchie (1952: 12) has recognized that many elements of Iroquois culture, especially ceramics, have wider distribution than across the Iroquois area. Yet at the same time he includes under the label of "Developmental Mohawk" the Kingston Site, which typologically is similar, but geographically is outside the historic Mohawk area.

MacNeish using the direct historical approach was not primarily concerned with identifying a site as Iroquois or Owasco. He started with sites assignable to a historic Iroquoian-speaking group and extended the identification back in time, connecting each site with its predecessor (MacNeish, 1952: 1). Theoretically, the lines of connection would end at the point where the ancestors of a tribe first entered the area. Practically, specific connections became lost in the early period of Iroquois development because of the decreasing number of connecting sites and artifacts as greater antiquity was involved, although general relationships were recognized with the earlier Point Peninsula. Consequently, it is still necessary to apply archaeological rather than tribal terminology to assemblages of considerable antiquity.

MacNeish (1952: 82) has used the term "Transitional Iroquois" in investigating the problem of Iroquois development and movements. While he does not define the term, he seems to mean sites typologically transitional between Iroquois and Owasco as well as temporally transitional. He restricts the term (but not explicitly) to material which was ancestral to that of known Iroquoian-speaking tribes.

In a second classification, MacNeish (Griffin, 1952: 46-58) has set up a number of foci for the New York area. He has related certain of these foci in a developmental sequence and has identified them with the historic Iroquois tribes. Since the data which form the basis for these foci and this tribal identification have not been published, and only a summary of their characteristics has been presented, it is difficult to use or to evaluate them. It is my impression that a number of the traits which he lists for particular foci have a wider distribution than the focus with which they are connected and hence cannot be considered diagnostic unless in a quantitative manner.

In Ontario, Emerson (n.d.: 236) has defined an (Ontario) Iroquois Aspect based on comparisons of traits or types of artifacts at fourteen sites. He lists five criteria common to these sites and definitive of the Iroquois Aspect. Four of these are general and would pertain to the Niagara Frontier sites as well as to most of the New York Iroquois sites. The fifth, location of villages generally on high, sandy plateaus near a river, would not allow inclusion of the Niagara Frontier sites or some others in New York. The first four criteria probably would not distinguish Iroquois sites in New York from pre-Iroquoian sites of the Owasco Aspect.

Two foci have been defined for the Ontario Iroquois Aspect, the Middleport Focus and the Roebuck Focus (Emerson, n.d.: 240). The foci are not identified with historic tribes. The sites of these foci as well as additional Iroquois sites in Ontario have been arranged by region in several temporal sequences, and the latest member of each sequence associated with a historic tribe with differing degrees of confidence (Emerson, n.d.: 255).

Each of the two approaches reflected in the classification of these archaeologists has its merits for particular problems. Most sites can be related to either classification. For example, the Otstungo Site can be classified as either Fonda Focus, Iroquois Aspect, or can be considered prehistoric Mohawk (Griffin, 1952: 51). There are, however, a few sites to which both classifications do not apply. Some sites will fall early in the sequence leading to a historic tribe and will share some traits of both the Owasco (or some other similar assemblage) and Iroquois Aspects. These sites cannot be classified as either Owasco

Aspect or Iroquois Aspect as these are presently defined. While they can be classified into foci, they cannot reliably be related to an Iroquois sequence derived from the direct historical approach. Other sites, like those of the Niagara Frontier, may be known to be Iroquois in historic times but because of the confusing ethnohistorical picture cannot be assigned to a tribal sequence. Thus, there is a residue of sites when classifications based on the two approaches are related.

The residue of sites can be reduced or, more important, utilized to increase our understanding of certain cultural processes, if certain questions are kept in mind to be investigated and future classifications devised to provide data bearing on them. Some of the questions which should be investigated are as follows: are there distinctive archaeological cultures (phases or foci) which can be identified with the historic tribes and their predecessors? Is there a distinctive archaeological culture which is associated with the Northern Iroquoian-speaking groups? Or have other cultural processes such as diffusion blurred any correspondence between the Iroquois as a whole or the individual tribes and distinctive archaeological cultures?

The first question, the identification of phases (foci) with historic tribes and their predecessors, has already received considerable investigation. MacNeish (Griffin, 1952: 51) has recognized a number of foci and has stated, "in many cases it is possible to connect these assemblages with artifact complexes found on sites which can be identified as historic tribal villages." He has then identified most of the foci with historic tribes and their prehistoric counterparts. While these identifications may be correct in most instances (the evidence has not been published), continuation along these same lines of methodology, i.e., linking foci without careful comparisons and subsequent interpretation of the formal relationship, will not clarify the question of the identification of phases with tribal localities.

Future investigations must take the course of continued regrouping of sites into phases on the basis of more and more precise comparisons of formal similarities. These comparisons need to be made across the entire Iroquois area and especially in peripheral areas. If a sufficiently high degree of similarity is selected as the basis for grouping the sites into phases or foci, then cultural differences which might be inferred to be the result of temporal factors will not obscure possible geographical differences. Instead, the result will be a larger number of phases consisting of fewer sites.

After phases have been defined, they must be correlated with one another. Rouse (1955: 714) has described the correlation of phases in terms of three relationships: descriptive, distributional, and genetic. In the first, "phases are grouped together because they share the same attributes, and hence each group reflects descriptive similarities among its constituent phases" (Rouse, 1955: 714). The descriptive correlation provides data for a variety of interpretations, but for purposes of the questions being investigated here, it is "a necessary prerequisite to proper correlation on the distributional and genetic levels" (Rouse, 1955: 715-16). The distributional correlation of phases requires their arrangement by temporal and spatial dimensions. Such a correlation of phases would provide the evidence for the association of distinctive archaeological cultures with tribal localities.

The occupation areas and even the exact village locations of many of the Iroquois tribes are well known in early historic times. As phases are located temporally and spatially, we can relate those phases which occurred in early historic times to known tribal areas to see whether the areas in which the sites of a phase are located coincide with tribal areas. Where this coincidence can be shown, the case for the identification of particular phases with historic tribes is greatly strengthened. In many instances, documentation of some components of the phase makes this identification a certainty. The identification of many early historic sites with particular tribes has already been done by MacNeish as part of the direct historical approach. The classification of sites into phases and attempted correlation of certain phases with tribal territories will still be necessary to investigate the question of whether tribal territories contain a distinctive artifact assemblage, or whether some components of a phase lie outside a particular tribal area.

Where the coincidence of all sites of a phase and tribal area does not occur, then we must re-examine the degree of formal similarity which was used in defining the phases to see whether all the components properly belong. If this is the case, then it will be necessary to seek other interpretations than tribal identity for the resemblances among the components of the phase, either as a group or individually. It is here that sites which are peripheral either to tribal territories or to the Iroquois area can provide a test of the usefulness of particular phases for making interpretations about tribal territories. For example, if a site like the Kingston Site (Ritchie, 1952) showed about the same number and kind of resemblances to other sites in Mohawk territory which would constitute a phase or focus and fewer resemblances to surrounding sites in the Hudson valley which would constitute a phase or focus, then a different interpretation such as its identification as a Mohawk village would be required from that which could be made if its resemblances were about equal to the diagnostic attributes of both phases.

The placement of phases along a temporal-spatial scale, Rouse (1955: 716) warns, does not indicate genetic connections. For example, if certain phases could be identified with historic tribes as outlined above, and other phases placed earlier with a corresponding tribal area distribution, these phases could not be considered on the basis of this arrangement to have any genetic connection with each other. Genetic connections must be established independently. A genetic or developmental relationship among phases is the least reliable correlation, according to Rouse (1955: 719), yet one which has been very frequently made by Iroquois archaeologists since this is the relationship of concern in tribal developments. Before reliable statements about tribal developments can be made, much more data must be analyzed and sites grouped into phases. The data should come from Early, Intermediate, and Historic sites across the entire Iroquois area. After phases have been arranged in a temporal-spatial framework, the genetic relationship among them can be investigated by showing which phase is most similar to which succeeding phase. For example, Phase A of the Early Period, Phase B of the Intermediate Period, and Phase C of the Historic Period occur in tribal area X. Phase D of the Early Period, Phase E of the Intermediate Period, and Phase F of the Historic Period occur in tribal area Y. If Phase B is more like Phase F than it is like Phase C, then Phase B is more likely to be genetically related to Phase F than are other phases which show fewer similarities to Phase F. It is still necessary to show that the diagnostic attributes of Phase F could have developed from those of Phase C. If a genetic relationship can be demonstrated, then a tribal movement from area X to area Y is indicated.

The second question of interest to future Iroquois studies is that of whether there is an association of culture type and culture area or subarea which can be identified as the Iroquois culture type and Iroquois culture area. This association of a distinctive cultural assemblage with a homogeneous geographical area should not be confused with the question of tribal territories and distinctive archaeological cultures. The investigation of the latter has been discussed in terms of the geographical relationship of phases and might result in statements about the territorial boundaries of the Iroquois people, compiled from statements about tribal territories. For example, if we can show that a certain phase represented Mohawk culture in early historic times, we can draw from those sites the approximate eastern boundary of the Iroquois at that time period. This is quite different from the identification of certain culture traits which singly or in association link the sites or phases across a homogeneous geographical area.

In the past, some anthropologists have stated that the early historic culture of Northern Iroquoian-speaking groups was sufficiently different from that of neighboring groups to warrant its distinction as a separate culture type or subculture type. The area of which this type is diagnostic is a subculture area (Wissler, 1938: 236; Kroeber, 1939: 89). Descriptions and explanations of these differences have not been made in detail, and there is not now general agreement on the distinctiveness of an Iroquois culture type (compare Fenton, 1940: 64 with Witthoft, 1951: 312).

The investigation of the question of whether there is an Iroquois culture type and Iroquois culture area must take place in two steps. First, the association of culture type with area must be demonstrated. Second, there must be a coincidence of this area with that in which Iroquoian-speaking people lived in early historic times. In practice, one may look for differences in the culture of the Iroquois compared to that of their neighbors in early historic times when the correlation of culture type and area can be studied from both archaeological and historical data. On this time level the spatial boundaries of diagnostic Iroquois culture traits must be delineated and examined to see if the area enclosed is a homogeneous geographical one without major barriers within and geographically distinct from surrounding areas. If this coincidence of diagnostic culture traits and geographical area can be shown, then an Iroquois culture type has been defined. Those distinctive attributes for which there is archaeological evidence can be traced back into earlier times in the archaeological culture which seems ancestral to that of the historic Iroquois. Approximately the same geographical boundaries should continue to define the subculture area as distinctive attributes are noted in the preceding archaeological culture.

As the data from earlier and earlier sites are examined for the distinctive attributes of the Iroquois culture type, changed forms of those attributes will be encountered and the term Iroquois culture type will no longer apply to those sites. Archaeologists working with material from these sites have recognized two classes of sites, one of which produces material called Iroquois and the other which produces material called Transitional or proto-Iroquois. These differences will lead to the definition of a second culture type, the Transitional Iroquois culture type. Again, the geographical area which this type occupies will have to be determined and tested for its geographical distinctiveness and compared with the boundaries of the Iroquois subculture area. Material from sites near but just outside the boundaries will have to be examined to test the discreteness of the boundaries.

Interpretations from the relationship of the Transitional Iroquois culture type to the Iroquois culture type will be useful for the problem of the origin of the Iroquois. Since the Transitional Iroquois type will be composed of a distinctive cluster of formal similarities shared by the sites composing it and distributed over a geographical area which remains to be discovered, the identification of sites of this type with Iroquoian-speaking people will require more care than the identification of sites of the Iroquois culture type with Iroquoian-speaking people. It is clear that sites which are now labeled Transitional Iroquois have forms which are intermediate between those found on Iroquois sites and those of an earlier culture such as the Owasco in central New York. There is no indication of a formal break preceding Iroquois culture in any part of the Iroquois area where the last pre-Iroquoian culture has been recognized. Nevertheless, the genetic relationship between the Iroquois culture type and Transitional Iroquois culture type will require continued study which will identify the cultural processes involved in the transition, such as migration or diffusion. Furthermore, the classification of sites with respect to Transitional Iroquois culture type must take into account sites which are geographically peripheral to the Iroquois area lest the explanation of change through migration be ruled out by the methodology.

It is not possible at this stage of research to test the usefulness of

"Iroquois culture type" and "Transitional Iroquois culture type" as outlined above or to give the diagnostic attributes of either. The present evidence indicates that there was a transition from Owasco or some related aspect to Iroquois as evidenced by many intermediate forms. This transition was probably of relatively short duration. Because of the numerous transitional forms, it may be impossible to find a complex of attributes, artifacts, or artifact types whose presence or absence will distinguish one culture type from the other. The differences between the culture types will probably be differences in the popularity of attributes. Since changes in the popularity of whatever diagnostic attributes are discovered would not have been simultaneous, one particular attribute with a specified frequency marks a significant point in the continuity of formal change. Using such an attribute as a marker, between the Transitional Iroquois culture type and the Iroquois culture type, other diagnostic differences between the two can be expressed in terms of relative frequency.

The most obvious difference between the Owasco Aspect and the Iroquois is to be found in pottery attributes, especially in techniques of rim decoration. Changes in the latter will distinguish the Transitional Iroquois culture type from the Iroquois culture type. The presence of some vessels showing incised rim decoration, together with other vessels showing either cord-wrapped stick, interrupted linear, dentate stamp, or all three techniques used for rim decoration, is diagnostic of sites of the Transitional Iroquois culture type. The Iroquois culture type, on the other hand, shows the presence of incised rim decoration, together with the absence of cord-wrapped stick, interrupted linear, and dentate stamp decoration.

The sites of the Niagara Frontier will be assigned to these culture types. In addition to the diagnostic attribute of rim decoration, other differences between the two culture types will be described. This diagnostic attribute is the criterion for classifying sites as one or the other culture type and should be applicable to sites throughout the Iroquois area. The other characteristics which will be described for each culture type distinguish one from the other only in the Niagara Frontier and will be modified as more data become available and as sites from other areas are considered.

The Transitional Iroquois Culture Type

Based on the data from only two sites, Oakfield and Kienuka, the Transitional Iroquois culture type in the Niagara Frontier shows the following pottery attributes:

1. Vessels with incised rim decoration occur in combination with vessels having rims decorated by any or all of the techniques of cord-wrapped stick, dentate stamp, or interrupted linear.
2. Approximately one fourth of the vessels are without collars.
3. Horizontal lines are the most popular motif of rim decoration.

4. Undecorated rims are relatively unpopular (less than 5 per cent).
5. Oblique and vertical motifs (Motifs 1, 2, and 3) decorate less than one-third of the rims.
6. Rim profile 5 occurs on approximately one-third of the collared vessels.
7. Neck decoration which is often a repetition of the collar decoration is popular.
8. Square castellations are absent.
9. Lip decoration of a single line encircling the mouth occurs on one-fifth to one-fourth of the vessels.

No attributes of the pipes, projectile points or settlement pattern can be noted as diagnostic of the Transitional Iroquois culture type.

Changes During the Early Period

During the time of the Transitional Iroquois culture type in the Niagara Frontier, certain changes were taking place in the time interval presumed to occur between the occupation of the Oakfield and Kienuka Sites. These changes become clear from differences between the pottery, pipes, and projectile points at Oakfield and Kienuka.

Probably the most noticeable change took place in the techniques of rim decoration. The cord-wrapped stick technique was common at Oakfield (16 per cent of all vessels), but it was completely missing at Kienuka, and the interrupted linear techniques also decreased from 14 per cent at Oakfield to 9 per cent at Kienuka. Incising increased between Oakfield and Kienuka, but the change away from cord-wrapped stick and interrupted linear was not entirely toward an increase in incising. At Kienuka there is an increased popularity (13 per cent compared to 5 per cent at Oakfield) in the use of punctations — rectangular, oval, and circular — to form the entire rim decoration. One wonders whether this is an outgrowth of the cord-wrapped stick impressed technique, since punctation seems closer to impressing than to incising, with the change occurring in the tool rather than in the motor habits required to execute the technique.

Several changes are noted in the popularity of certain motifs which decorated the rims of pottery vessels. Using figures for the frequency of incised motifs (Table III) among all technique and motif combinations (totals of Tables III and IV), there are changes in incised Motifs 9 and 13, and 1, 2, and 3 which may be related changes. At Oakfield, Motif 9, horizontal lines, was the most popular. Motif 13, vertical lines above horizontal lines, occurred with low frequency (4 per cent), while Motifs 1, 2, and 3, oblique and vertical lines, were absent (0.8 per cent) at Oakfield. At Kienuka, Motif 9 decreased in frequency by 20 per cent, indicating that horizontal lines had passed the peak of their popularity. Motif 13 doubled in popularity, occurring at Kienuka on 8 per cent of the combinations of technique and motif. Motifs 1, 2, and 3 show the greatest change, a combined increase to 31 per cent of the total combinations.

Thus, during the Early Period horizontal lines decreased while vertical and oblique lines, alone (Motifs 1, 2, and 3) and above horizontal lines (Motif 13) increased. I suggest that Motif 13 is formally intermediate between Motif 9 and Motifs 1, 2, and 3 and that one manifestation of the change from Motif 9 to Motifs 1, 2, and 3 is the intermediate form, Motif 13. In Ontario, the change of decreasing popularity in Motif 9 took a different form. In the pottery type Ontario Oblique the horizontal lines of the rim extended onto the neck. They continued as neck decoration in the pottery type Pound Necked while the rim motif changed to Motifs 1, 2, and 3 (MacNeish, 1952: 14, 16). Motif 6, opposed incised lines, appeared for the first time at Kienuka. During the latter part of the Early Period all the motifs which attained any degree of popularity during the rest of the sequence are present.

In rim profile, convex interiors on collared vessels were scarce at Oakfield (2 per cent), but came into greater use at Kienuka with increases in Profiles 7 and 8 (18 per cent). This increase is related to decreases in Profile 1 and Profile 4 between Oakfield and Kienuka. This change in Profile 1 is not part of any discernible trend since the popularity of Profile 1 fluctuates through time. The decrease in Profile 4 is largely in the fourth variant of this profile (Fig. 13), a form closely related to Owasco beaded lip and one which rarely occurs later in the sequence.

In projectile points a marked change in width and somewhat less change in length occurred during the Early Period. By the end of the Early Period the pattern of projectile point length was well fixed, but width continued to decrease slightly during much of the following period. Traditional Iroquois pipe styles appeared for the first time in the Early Period at Kienuka, where the decorated rimmed trumpet and the ring bowl (form unknown) were found. The Oakfield pipes are still in the tradition of some earlier Owasco-like culture.

The Early Period and its Antecedents

The Oakfield Site

The Oakfield Site has been classified as Transitional Iroquois and assigned to the Early Period. It is the earliest known representative of the Iroquois tradition in the area and, as previously mentioned, shares with the earlier Owasco culture in other parts of the state a number of ceramic, pipe, and projectile point attributes. In ceramics the Oakfield Site has the following attributes which also appear on Owasco pottery as described by Ritchie and MacNeish (1949):

Cord-wrapped stick impressed pottery decoration
Interrupted linear pottery decoration
Cord-marked body sherds
Lip decoration by cord-wrapped stick crossing lip obliquely

Short, oblique,cord-wrapped stick impressions at base of collar
Rim interior decoration made by incising or cord-wrapped stick
Plats on the neck made by cord-wrapped stick impressions
Beaded lips
Similar forms of castellations
Rim motifs of horizontal and oblique lines
Cord-wrapped stick impressions over cord-malleated rim area
Vessel form (based on two vessels only)
Encircling row of short, oblique, cord-wrapped stick impressions on the shoulder

All these attributes except the last occur on sites of both the Castle Creek and Canandaigua foci of the Owasco Aspect. Dentate stamping, present in small numbers at Oakfield, does not occur in the Castle Creek and Canandaigua foci (Ritchie and MacNeish, 1949: 120).

It is more difficult to point out Oakfield vessels which are clearly modifications of specific Owasco styles. Many of the Oakfield vessels having such Owasco features as interrupted linear or cord-wrapped stick impressions are in other respects quite Iroquois-like; for example, vessels of Iroquois shape and decorative motif may have the horizontal lines decorating the collars executed in the interrupted linear technique instead of the incising of later periods. The vessels which do resemble Owasco types more closely are usually collarless, have outflaring rims decorated with cord-wrapped stick impressions arranged in oblique lines, and show cord-wrapped paddle stamping as a surface finish on the rim. Although they are not identical with any Owasco vessels, they can hardly be described as Iroquois in any respect and raise a suspicion of either trade or a double occupation at the site. There are collarless vessels at Oakfield, however, with incised decoration over corded-paddle surface finish which help to fill the gap between the virtually Iroquois and the virtually Owasco pots and consequently to favor the single occupation interpretation.

The pipes at Oakfield resemble Owasco pipes in two respects, cord-wrapped stick impressed decoration and a bulging bowl. The bulging bowl is evidenced by two small fragments which indicate a shape similar to some of the pipes from the Owasco Aspect (Ritchie, 1944: 30). The projectile points at Oakfield are longer and wider than those from later sites and thus are more like those of the Owasco Aspect.

Possible Antecedents in the Area

There is some evidence which suggests that a Late Woodland culture earlier than that represented at Oakfield is present in the Niagara Frontier. This evidence consists of rim sherds collected from the surface by A. L. Benedict from several sites in the city of Buffalo which are now destroyed and from Fort Erie, Ontario, where the exact site location is unclear. Ritchie has very kindly examined at my request some of these rim sherds from Fort Erie and noted their resemblance to sherds from Jacks Reef and Wickham of Point Peninsula 4 and Carpenter Brook of the Owasco Aspect (personal correspondence, 1954). The resemblances are general rather than specific. Other rim sherds are, in my opinion, typologically closer to Transitional Iroquois sherds from the Oakfield Site, but unless larger samples become available from sites that are village settlements, the relationship of these rim sherds to a Niagara Frontier Iroquois development from some local pre-Iroquoian culture remains in question. The presence of pre-Iroquoian sherds does not necessarily point to a local development.

The Niagara Frontier lies between areas to the east and west in which pre-Iroquoian complexes are recognized and considered by some archaeologists to be ancestral to local Iroquois developments in those areas. To the east is the Owasco Aspect; to the west in Ontario is the Glen Meyer Focus, which will be discussed later. Rim sherds from the Niagara Frontier which appear to be earlier than the Oakfield Site resemble some pottery from both of these neighboring complexes. These sherds in the Niagara Frontier may have had their source in one or both of these other complexes, or they may belong to some similar complex in the Niagara Frontier.

The Iroquois Culture Type

In the Niagara Frontier the following pottery attributes or attribute frequencies distinguish the Iroquois culture type as it is found at the Shelby, Buffam, Eaton, Goodyear, and Green Lake Sites:

1. Incised decorations occur on over 80 per cent of the vessel rims.
2. Rims decorated by the cord-wrapped stick and interrupted linear techniques are absent.
3. Uncollared vessels constitute less than one-fifth of the total.
4. The horizontal line motif is found on less than 3 per cent of the rims of decorated vessels.
5. Over half of the decorated vessel rims bear a motif of oblique and vertical lines.
6. Rim profile 5 is found on less than 15 per cent of the collared vessels.
7. Fifteen per cent or more of the castellations are square.
8. Neck decoration is infrequent or absent.
9. Lip decoration of a single line encircling the mouth of a vessel is absent.

There are no attributes of the pipes or projectile points which set off the Iroquois culture type in the Niagara Frontier from the Transitional Iroquois culture type.

Changes During the Intermediate Period

The beginning of the Intermediate Period coincides with the beginning of the Iroquois culture type. Included in this period are the Shelby Site, the Buffam Street Site, and the Eaton Site, which are the sources for statements about changes during the early, middle, and late parts of the Intermediate Period. Early in the Intermediate Period there was an increase in the number of collared vessels which reach an equilibrium after the Shelby Site and show only slight fluctuations thereafter. It is more difficult to characterize the rim profile changes during the Intermediate Period, for there is considerable fluctuation and many slight changes in frequency. Profile 13 was introduced at the beginning of the Intermediate, but later waned in frequency. No new profiles attained any measure of popularity during this period. The increase in well defined collars with concave interiors continued, and convex interiors became more numerous.

At the beginning of the Intermediate Period at the Shelby Site incising achieved its peak of 94 per cent. It decreased to 84 per cent at the end of the period, not because of competition from other decorative techniques but rather because fewer vessels were decorated. Several motifs changed in popularity during the Intermediate Period. Motif 3, vertical lines, had its greatest popularity during this time, having increased at the beginning of the period and decreased toward the end. Motif 6, opposed lines, had high popularity during the early part of the Intermediate Period at the Shelby Site. This was the only time when opposed lines were more popular than simple obliques or verticals (Motifs 1, 2, 3). Motif 8, which perhaps developed from Motif 6 by leaving a space between the opposed lines, occurred mainly at Buffam in the middle of the Intermediate. Combining Motifs 6 and 8 to consider opposed decoration in general, there was a more gradual change: Shelby, 37 per cent; Buffam, 18 per cent; Eaton, 12 per cent. Toward the end of the Intermediate Period after the Eaton Site, this decrease leveled off and little change took place in the succeeding period. The addition of punctations to an incised design was present at the beginning of the Intermediate Period, as a continuation from the latter part of the Early Period. The punctations were placed at the base of the collar or immediately below the base. Their frequency was 39 per cent at the beginning of the Intermediate, and they decreased to 7 per cent at the end of the period.

Notches in the exterior edge of the lip where it joined the collar were frequent in the early part of the Intermediate. They occurred almost entirely on decorated rims, as very few rims during the early part of the Intermediate were undecorated. The popularity of this notching decreased sharply during the Intermediate. There was a greater width of rims at the Shelby Site, where 18 per cent are over an inch in width. Most of these wider rims had incipient collars, or no collars, and the wide decorated areas were filled with opposed triangular blocks of broad, shallow incised lines. This combination of wide rim, incipient collar, and opposed decoration continued at Buffam to a lesser extent and was gone by the end of the Intermediate.

Squared castellations made their first appearance at the beginning of the Intermediate and gained in popularity throughout the rest of the sequence. The addition of a vertical ridge with punctations beneath castellations is confined to the Shelby and Buffam Sites and accordingly is a characteristic of the early Intermediate Period.

The pipe forms of the Intermediate Period consisted of the well-known Iroquois trumpet, square bowl, and effigy shapes. Plain trumpet pipes were limited to Buffam and Eaton and may turn out to be a temporal marker here as in Ontario. Human face effigies occurred at Shelby and Buffam, but animal effigies are limited to the Buffam and Eaton Sites. An important change was the appearance of barrel and vasiform stone pipes at the end of the period at the Eaton Site. Projectile points had a relatively uniform average length throughout the period, but the width fluctuated.

Changes During the Historic Period

Changes in ceramics between the end of the Intermediate Period and the beginning of the Historic Period were very slight. This near identity at the Eaton and Goodyear Sites suggests a short-time interval. More changes occurred between the Goodyear and the Green Lake Sites during the Historic Period.

Well-defined collars with convex interiors (Profile 7) showed the most increase at the end of the sequence; their frequency at Green Lake is about double that in earlier times. There seems to have been a greater variety in rim profiles at the beginning of the Historic Period than at any other time, judging from the greater frequency of atypical profiles at Goodyear. On the other hand, the decorative motifs showed more variety at Green Lake than at any other site except those of the Early Period. This variability appears to be related to the decrease in plain vessels at the same time. Undecorated vessels were increasing during the Intermediate Period and attained maximum popularity early in the Historic Period. They decreased again at Green Lake, and two new motifs, 7 and 10, are popular for the first time. Punctations at the bottom of the collar increased during the Historic Period after a previous decrease, but now occurred mainly on otherwise plain rims. A similar trend occurred in the notches at the junction of the lip and collar.

It remains to note only certain new features which appeared during the Historic Period, probably as a result of outside influence from Ontario. These are carinated shoulders and complex shoulder decoration, which occur for the first time at the Green Lake Site. It is difficult to estimate the frequencies of these attributes, although they are not plentiful and may even result from imported vessels. These new attributes are important as an indication of increased contacts outside the area. Notable changes in the pipes during the Historic Period were the addition of the acorn ring bowl and the absence of the plain trumpet, both of which may prove to be markers for this period.

Other sites occur in the Niagara Frontier which certainly fill some of the intervals in the sequence, but they are represented by very small samples and are difficult to interpret. One seems to belong to the Intermediate Period and several to the Historic Period. It seems probable that the area was occupied more or less continuously from the Early Period on.

In discussing the geography of the Niagara Frontier and the presence of sites only on the Huron and Erie Plains, it was pointed out that historical as well as geographic factors might account for the absence of sites in the Allegheny Plateau Section. Sites of the Early and Intermediate Periods are north and in three cases west of those in the Historic Period. This geographical segregation is borne out by what I know of other sites not considered here. An exception is the contact site on Grand Island which has been called Neutral. Their distribution suggests that there was at least one slow movement of villages south and east from Buffalo during the Historic Period so that the later villages were closest to the foothills of the Allegheny Plateau. It remains for future investigation to test whether the movement stopped short of the Allegheny Plateau because of the unfavorable environment or whether particular historical events such as those discussed in the ethnohistory resulted in an abandonment of the area later in the Historic Period.

In summary, in the absence of any reliable technique for assigning absolute dates to the sites in the Niagara Frontier Iroquois sequence, three periods have been recognized, the Early, Intermediate, and Historic. The Oakfield and Kienuka Sites are of the Early Period. Shelby, Buffam Street, and Eaton are of the Intermediate, and Goodyear and Green Lake are of the Historic. The Goodyear Site was probably occupied sometime during the interval 1550-1600 A.D. and the Green Lake Site during 1575-1625 A.D.

The sites of the Niagara Frontier sequence are judged to exhibit two culture types which I have designated Transitional Iroquois and Iroquois. Transitional Iroquois occurs during the Early Period, and the formal marker for both is the presence of incised pottery rim decoration in combination with cord-wrapped stick, interrupted linear, or dentate stamp rim decoration. The Iroquois culture type which lacks cord-wrapped stick, interrupted linear, or dentate stamp rim decoration occurs during both the Intermediate and Historic Periods, which are separated by the absence or presence of European trade goods. The characteristics of the Transitional Iroquois and Iroquois culture types in the Niagara Frontier have been given. In contrast to these characteristics which are general descriptions of the local material culture during these periods are the changes which occurred during each period.

IX

COMPARISONS AND CONCLUSIONS

The sites of the Niagara Frontier Iroquois sequence will now be compared to Iroquois sites from surrounding areas. The framework for the comparisons will be the time periods, Early, Intermediate, and Historic, which have been recognized in the Niagara Frontier by certain diagnostic formal attributes. When these attributes occur on sites outside the Niagara Frontier, those sites will be considered to be the same time period as the local ones. I will then compare material from sites of the same period in two areas to note regional similarities and differences, first to the north, then to the south, and finally to the east. The use of the terms, Early, Intermediate, and Historic, is consistent in this section with their definition earlier in this paper. My use may differ from the temporal designations of other archaeologists for the same sites. If I am referring to temporal designations other than my own, this will be indicated.

Comparisons to the North

Throughout this paper frequent references have been made to similarities between the material of Niagara Frontier sites and Iroquois sites of Ontario. One reason for this is the greater number of published and unpublished reports on Canadian sites in recent years; not only is there more information from Ontario, but also the data are presented in more comparable terms. In making further comparisons between the Niagara Frontier sites and those of Ontario, the similarities and differences which I shall note are impressions from examinations of Canadian collections and from statements in published accounts. Judgments on the basis of impressions often cannot be supported when data as homogeneous as those from western Iroquois sites undergo more thorough analysis.

Sites in western and central Ontario fall into two groups, those of the Peninsula and those north of the Peninsula. The Ontario Peninsula sequence will be discussed first, starting with the Uren Site, mentioning its antecedents, and then proceeding from the Uren Site forward in time.

One major difference between Niagara Frontier and Ontario sites of both groups is the form of projectile points from the Early Period on. Many of the Ontario Iroquois sites have produced triangular points with side notches (Emerson, n.d.: 233), as well as unnotched triangles. Notched triangles do not occur in the Niagara Frontier.

In the Ontario Peninsula sequence, the Uren Site (Wintemberg, 1928;

MacNeish, 1952: 12) falls in the Early Period and shows the greatest similarities to the Oakfield Site. Oakfield has a higher frequency of cord-wrapped stick impressed pottery rims (16 per cent cf. 2 per cent), a similar frequency of interrupted linear rims (13 per cent cf. 15 per cent), and less dentate-stamped rims (1 per cent cf. 4 per cent). The nodes on both pottery and pipes at Uren are absent at Oakfield, except for one potsherd. The incised horizontal rim motif is more frequent at Uren. Oakfield pottery has more collars and fewer grooved paddled bodies. The similarities of the two sites indicate near contemporaneity within the Early Period.

Across a restricted area in the Ontario Peninsula from Long Point, Lake Erie, and Ipperwash, Lake Huron, are remains of a group of sites which Lee (1959: 90) has grouped into the Glen Meyer Focus. Both Lee and Ridley (1958: 22) consider these sites ancestral to those of the Uren Focus. In 1954 through the courtesy of Lee, I made an examination of some of the material in the National Museum of Canada's collections from the Glen Meyer sites. Some of the Glen Meyer pottery resembled those few rim sherds from the Niagara Frontier which have been mentioned previously as earlier than Oakfield.

Other sites in the Ontario Peninsula — Middleport (Wintemberg, 1948), Pound (Emerson, n.d.: 240), Southwold (MacNeish, 1952: 12), and Lawson (Wintemberg, 1939) — all belong to the Intermediate Period. Middleport and Pound show close similarities to Kienuka of the Early Period, the resemblance being stronger in the case of Middleport. The diagnostic pottery attribute, interrupted linear technique, which places Kienuka in the Early Period, is absent at Middleport and Pound. Both have pottery with horizontal neck decoration (Pound Necked), lower frequencies of incised vertical and oblique rim decoration, and higher frequencies of criss-cross designs and horizontal motifs (MacNeish, 1952: 12) than Kienuka.

MacNeish (1952: 12) has included the Southwold Earthworks in his Neutral sequence. Between the Pound Site and the Southwold Earthworks changes occur which resemble those between Kienuka and Shelby. Horizontal motifs decrease sharply, and incised vertical and oblique lines increase sharply. On the other hand, opposed decoration, one of the distinguishing characteristics of the early part of the Intermediate Period in the Niagara Frontier, was not as popular in Ontario.

The Lawson Site (Wintemberg, 1939) resembles both Buffam Street and Eaton. It is closer to Eaton in the frequency of undecorated rim sherds, opposed rim decoration, and stone vasiform pipes. No Historic Period sites have been related to the sequence from the Ontario Peninsula, although such sites do occur (Ridley, 1959: 11).

In Ontario north of the Peninsula and generally north of Lake Ontario, more Iroquois sites have been carefully investigated than in any other part of the Iroquois area. These sites which number at least fifteen are spread over an area from Georgian Bay on the west to Montreal on the east, but concentrate between Toronto and Georgian Bay.

The closest resemblances to the Niagara Frontier occur on the earliest levels.

The Barrie Site (Ridley, 1958), an Early Period Site in Simcoe County, has produced material very similar to that from Uren. The sherd sample which Ridley (1958: 22) salvaged from the Barrie Site is small, and precise comparisons with the Oakfield material are of limited value. It is clear that incising is much less common and interrupted linear much more common at Barrie than at Oakfield and Uren. Cord-wrapped stick impressed rim decoration is absent at Barrie.

Ridley (1958) has also described material from the Boys Site near Toronto and has discussed its ancestral relationships to the Barrie artifacts. The Boys Site is closely related to the Glen Meyer Focus (Ridley, 1958: 22) whose semblance to some Niagara Frontier pottery has been noted.

The Webb Site (Ridley, 1952) in Simcoe County is similar to the Kienuka Site. The presence of interrupted linear decoration on rim sherds places it in the Early Period.

Three sites in the Humber Valley, Black Creek, Downsview, and Parsons (Emerson, n.d.: 255; 1956: 37; 1959: 98-107), are of the Intermediate Period. There is a higher percentage of horizontal incised rim decoration at Black Creek (Ontario Horizontal 12 per cent) than at any Niagara Frontier site during the Intermediate Period. A few sherds from Black Creek resemble pottery from Shelby and Buffam, but on the whole the neck decoration in central Ontario gives the pottery a very different appearance. The presence of plain trumpet pipes at Buffam and Eaton link these temporally with Downsview and Black Creek.

Specific similarities between the sites of the prehistoric Lalonde Focus (Ridley, 1952) in Simcoe County and any sites of the Niagara Frontier are lacking. The large vessels with wide collars which distinguish the Lalonde Focus do not occur in the Niagara Frontier. The Lalonde trumpet pipe, a plain trumpet of unusual size, is found in reduced size at Buffam and Eaton, as well as at numerous other sites throughout the Iroquois area. The presence of the plain trumpet pipe is evidence for the assignment of the Lalonde Focus to the Intermediate Period.

Resemblances between the Niagara Frontier Iroquois sites and the Sidey-MacKay, KcKenzie, Aurora, and Benson Sites of central Ontario are general. The presence of European trade goods on these sites places them in the Historic Period. Their similarities with Niagara Frontier sites of Goodyear and Green Lake consist of shared pipe classes such as the acorn ring bowl and identical pottery rim decorative motifs. The difference between these four Ontario Iroquois sites and those of the Niagara Frontier are most noticeable in the frequencies of particular motifs of pottery rim decoration. For example, the popularity of plain rims with and without punctations at the base of the collar is greater in the Niagara Frontier. Neck decoration, complex shoulder decoration, and carinated shoulders are frequent on Ontario pottery of the Historic Period, yet absent in the Niagara Frontier. Finally, a comparison of the list of decorative motifs on pottery rims shows that all motifs used on Historic Niagara Frontier sites also occur on these four Ontario sites. Several motifs, however, which were popular on these Historic Ontario sites do not occur on Niagara Frontier Iroquois Sites of the same period.

In summary, the material from Ontario Iroquois sites is very like that from Niagara Frontier Iroquois sites. The closest relationship exists on the earliest level. Changes in pottery decoration are parallel for many attributes. In general, the Niagara Frontier material lacks certain distinctive attributes which occur on Ontario sites. These are side-notched, triangular projectile points and nodes, complex neck and shoulder decoration, and carinated shoulders on pottery vessels. All Niagara Frontier Iroquois attributes are shared with Ontario sites, differing only in their popularities.

Comparisons to the South

South of the Niagara Frontier are several sites which Guthe (1958) has recently studied. He has pointed out the inadequacies of the data and the problems of drawing conclusions about their chronological position. The absence of information on the frequency of pottery types makes precise comparisons out of the question. Only four southwestern New York sites, Westfield, Burning Springs, Silverheels, and Ripley, will be compared here.

Two outstanding differences in the Iroquois pottery from the two areas seem to exist on all time levels. South of the Niagara Frontier, there is a greater percentage of shell tempering and vessel body roughening by cord-wrapped or grooved paddle. Guthe (1958: 39) has pointed out that these differences probably result from stronger Monongahela Woodland influences in southwestern New York. The distribution of shell-tempered pottery, except for infrequent sherds, is restricted to an area south of Cattaraugus Creek. Roughened vessel bodies, which are frequent on all Late Woodland and Early Historic sites south of the Niagara Frontier, occur frequently in the Niagara Frontier only during the Early Period.

Some pottery vessels from the Westfield Site bear out Guthe's (1958: 40) observation that one occupation at the Westfield Site is an early Iroquois one with relationships to the north. The form, decorative techniques, and motifs of certain Westfield vessels are very similar to some from Oakfield. On this basis I would assign part of the Westfield material to the Early Period.

The Burning Springs Site (Parker, 1922: 162-181) on Cattaraugus Creek is difficult to assign to any part of the time sequence. From an examination of the small collection at the New York State Museum, the majority of sherds resemble those from Oakfield and Kienuka, while a few looked more like some from Eaton. Noticeably absent were simple, incised vertical, and oblique lines in quantity. A high proportion of simple, incised vertical, and oblique lines characterizes the pottery of the Niagara Frontier Iroquois sequence throughout the Intermediate and Historic Periods.

Perhaps the most difficult problem is how a site so near (about 30 miles) to the Niagara Frontier Iroquois sites could have large amounts of shell-tempered and cord-wrapped paddled bodies and show so little influence on the Niagara Frontier. Two explanations occur to me as most likely. First, the Burning Springs Site may have been occupied during some part of the Intermediate Period not represented by the known Niagara Frontier sites. Second, the Burning Springs Site may have been occupied during the Early Period when contemporary sites in the Niagara Frontier may have been in the northern portion of the area. At least the two Early Period sites known at present are in the northern section of the Niagara Frontier. Under those conditions the greater distance of Niagara Frontier sites from Burning Springs might account for the weak influences. Furthermore cord-marked bodies on pottery vessels were in fashion during the Early Period in the Niagara Frontier with the result that influences from Burning Springs on body treatment would not be observable in the Niagara Frontier. At present there is no evidence which allows a choice of one or the other of these explanations.

The Silverheels Site (Houghton, 1920: 44; Parker, 1922: 207) has been thought to be a Seneca village after 1655 A.D. Guthe (1958: 52) suggested the presence of two occupations because of the presence of "Neutral-Wenro" pottery with Seneca Barbed Collar vessels. The absence of guns, whole brass kettles, and Jesuit material in sixty-five burials indicates to me that a date around 1640 A.D. is more in accord with the dates for changes in European trade material in the Seneca sequence (Wray and Schoff, 1953). If a date as early as 1640 is accepted, then the identification of the site with the Seneca is in question since there is no record of Seneca villages in the Niagara Frontier at this time, and the main Seneca villages were south of Rochester. Descriptions of the pottery vessels are too incomplete to allow careful comparisons with material from the Niagara Frontier Iroquois sites to which the Silverheels Site must eventually be related. The assignment of the bulk of the cultural material to the Historic Period is clear.

Problems presented by the Ripley Site are similar to those of the Silverheels Site. In many respects artifacts from it resemble material from Goodyear, and MacNeish (1952: 22) considered Goodyear ancestral to Ripley. MacNeish analyzed the Ripley Site material in the Peabody Museum, while I examined only that in the New York State Museum. In the latter collection, two occupations may be represented at the Ripley Site to judge by a higher frequency of cord-marked and grooved-paddle body sherds at Ripley than at Goodyear. On the other hand, this may result from Monongahela Woodland influences (Mayer-Oakes, 1955: 155-62). Certainly part of the cultural material at Ripley is temporally close to the Goodyear Site and belongs to the Historic Period.

Comparisons have been made between the Niagara Frontier Iroquois sites and four villages to the south, Westfield, Burning Springs, Silverheels, and Ripley. The condition of the information from the sites to the south makes precise comparison difficult since the frequency of artifact types is unknown. There is a noticeable similarity of pottery and other artifacts in the two areas. The outstanding difference is the higher proportion of shell-tempered and roughened vessel bodies on pottery in the south. The Westfield and Burning Springs Sites are prehistoric; the Silverheels and Ripley Sites are of the Historic Period.

Comparisons to the East

In the area immediately to the east of the Niagara Frontier, no distinction will be made between those pre-Contact Period sites which have been placed in the Seneca sequence and those which have been placed in the Cayuga sequence. Here three sites can be called Transitional in type and presumably are Early Period in date. They are Hummel, Dansville, and Long Point (Guthe, 1955; MacNeish, 1952: 48-49; Wright, 1950). On the basis of the presence of cord-wrapped stick impressions on the pottery, all resemble Oakfield more closely than Kienuka. If all the material from the Hummel Site is attributable to a single occupation for a limited period of time, then it represents a Transitional type closer to Owasco than does the Oakfield Site, on the basis of techniques of pottery decoration. Owasco pottery types account for over half of the sherds at Hummel. Interrupted linear occurs somewhat more frequently than at Oakfield (15 per cent cf. 9 per cent). Incising is much less frequent (7 per cent cf. 49 per cent). Horizontal motifs in the several techniques dominate (MacNeish, 1952: 40). The collars in general appear to be less developed than at Oakfield.

The Dansville material is not familiar to me except for the pottery types given by MacNeish (1952: 40), who considered it ancestral to Long Point. The Long Point Site had multiple occupations, and I am uncertain what criteria MacNeish used for recognizing those sherds attributable to the Transitional type. In contrast to Oakfield, both the Hummel and Long Point Sites had fragments of trumpet pipes decorated with cord-wrapped stick impressions. Dansville and Long Point pottery had more dentate stamp and cord-wrapped stick impressions, and less interrupted linear decoration than did Oakfield. No site in the Seneca-Cayuga area shows specific similarity to Kienuka.

Two sites presumably of the Intermediate Period, Belcher and Richmond Mills (Reed Fort) (MacNeish, 1952: 48), show resemblances to the Shelby Site. All three have high frequencies of opposed decoration on collars, high collars, and use of punctations with incised lines to form the decorations. Belcher is considered by MacNeish to be ancestral to Reed Fort and has lower, less well-developed collars than the latter. In this feature it resembles Shelby somewhat more than does Richmond Mills. On the other hand, neither of these eastern sites has as many low collars with simple incised decoration as Shelby. The LeRoy Fort (Parker, 1922: 310-13) also appears related to this group.

The precontact Seneca sequence is poorly known, but on the historic level it is one of the most thoroughly understood of any Iroquois tribal sequence. Similarities between the Seneca sites and those of the Niagara Frontier are most noticeable among the pipes. The closest resemblance in pottery occurs at the Adams Site (Wray and Schoff, 1953) which yields the earliest European trade goods. As the Seneca specialization of a heavy, notched collar developed more fully, the resemblances are less. They are strongest between Adams and Goodyear, and I think these sites are of about the same time period.

Further east, the sites of the Onondaga-Oneida and the Mohawk show fewer similarities, especially on the historic levels. I shall mention only a few of those sites which I shall compare with the Transitional sites of the Early Period in the Niagara Frontier.

In the Niagara Frontier, the presence of the cord-wrapped stick, dentate stamp, and interrupted linear techniques used in rim decoration was the basis for the assignment of sites to the Early Period. It was noted that the dominant pottery decorative technique of this period was horizontal lines. These same criteria have been useful in comparing sites in western Ontario, in southwestern New York, and eastward across New York. An examination of these pottery attributes on sites of the Onondaga-Oneida sequence in northern New York indicates that changes in pottery decorative techniques and motifs there were not parallel to those in the Niagara Frontier (unless the small sample size from several northern sites makes parts of that sequence open to question). On the basis of the presence of cord-wrapped stick and dentate stamp decoration, northern sites assignable to the Early Period are Ivey, Lanorie, Swarthout, Durfee, and Roebuck from early to late. There may be disagreement with the assignment of some of the above members to the Early Period, since MacNeish (1952: 56) has placed Durfee and Roebuck in late prehistoric times. The time period which I am using are relative ones established on the basis of certain typological criteria, and I prefer to be consistent in my assignment of sites, recognizing that the Durfee and Roebuck sites might not belong to the same time period now designated "Early" if absolute dates were available. My impression is that these two sites are probably later than the remainder of the Early Period sites.

Throughout the Early Period in northern New York, dentate stamping is more popular than other nonincised techniques. The cord-wrapped stick technique is second in popularity and lasts throughout most of the Early Period. Interrupted linear, which in the western area lasts the longest and dominates other nonincised techniques towards the end of the Early Period, is popular only at the Ivey Site. Apparently it died out quickly, before the time when dentate stamping reached a peak (at the Lanorie Site, 28 per cent). Horizontal incised decoration did not become as popular in the north as in the west and reached greatest popularity before the ascent of dentate stamping took place in the north.

In the Mohawk area there are four sites of the Chance Horizon (Ritchie, 1952) which are regarded as developmental Mohawk and which belong to the Early Period. At the earliest site, Oak Hill, 44 per cent of the sherds were decorated with cord-wrapped stick impressions, and this frequency decreased to 6 per cent at the latest site of the Horizon. Cord impressions outlasted interrupted linear stamping which was popular (19 per cent) only on the earliest site, Oak Hill. The persistence of cord impressions compared to interrupted linear is similar to the situation in northern New York and differs from the western area, where interrupted linear continued later than cord impressions from the evidence of the Kienuka Site.

In the Chance Horizon, cord-marked body sherds were never as popular as at the Oakfield Site, and check-stamped sherds were probably more frequent (2 per cent), although exact figures are not available from sites of the Niagara Frontier. It seems that cord-marked body treatment was being replaced by smooth body treatment more rapidly in eastern New York than in western New York during the Early Period. Perhaps the source of the stimulus which produced body smoothing was closer to the Mohawk area than to western New York.

Two conclusions have been reached by comparing techniques of rim decoration and vessel body treatment in eastern and western New York during the Early Period. First, cord-wrapped stick impressed rims persisted longer in the east than in the west. Second, cord-marked bodies went out of style earlier in the east than in the west.

The Mohawk area is the only one where figures are available to compare the changing frequencies of cord-marked bodies and cord-wrapped stick impressed rims during the Early Period. It is clear that cord-marked bodies (3 per cent for the Horizon) were never as popular as cord-wrapped stick impressed rims (a range from 30 per cent to 6 per cent throughout the Horizon). It is generally accepted that the rim decoration and the body treatment were both made by the same tool, a cord-wrapped paddle. It is rather unexpected to find that changes in the frequencies with which the two areas of a pottery vessel were so decorated were not occurring simultaneously.

The absence of dentate stamping as a technique of rim decoration at the Chance Horizon sites is also unexpected, especially in the light of the postulated origin of part of the Mohawk culture in the St. Lawrence area (Ritchie, 1952: 27) where we noted high numbers of dentate-stamped rims during the Early Period.

The horizontal line motif was less frequent in the Mohawk area than in western New York, although exact figures are not available for Mohawk rims. Mohawk shoulder designs are more complex. Opposed line decorations, usually in triangular areas, are frequent on the wide collars, whereas they are absent in the Niagara Frontier during the Early Period.

Pipes from Chance Horizon sites display more of the traditional Iroquois forms than are found on Early sites in the Niagara Frontier. The ring bowl and trumpet pipe are found frequently, whereas only a single ring bowl and trumpet have been found at Kienuka and none at Oakfield. Among the later sites of the horizon, plain trumpets, effigy forms, and square top bowls occur. These forms have not been found until the Intermediate Period in Western New York, and they are regarded as occurring at about the same time in the Ontario sequence. Future investigations must determine whether the diagnostic pottery decorating techniques of the Early Period in the Niagara Frontier lasted later in the Mohawk Valley, or whether pipe forms of the Intermediate Period in the west appeared earlier in the Mohawk Valley.

Outside the area of the Iroquoian-speaking people, specific similarities do not exist with the exception of the ceramics in immediately adjacent areas, mainly to the east and south. These similarities are regarded as either the result of Iroquois influence or as part of a general trend in the Late Woodland of the Northeast (MacNeish, 1952: 85-88). Many of the artifact types or attributes associated with the Iroquois are widespread in the Northeast, for the Iroquois shared in certain major developments taking place across the Eastern United States during the Late Woodland Period (Griffin, 1946: 92). On the other hand, the Iroquois culture type will be found to consist of a unique clustering or at least frequencies of artifact types.

During the Late Woodland Period there were general and widespread trends toward smooth, globular bodies on vessels, incised decoration, plain rims, shell tempering, appendages on vessels, and effigy forms. A number of cultures in the Northeast and the Ohio Valley shared in certain of these traits. The absence of some of these traits in various Late Woodland cultures look like rejection rather than ignorance, for it seems likely that most had contact with all these new ideas. Thus the Iroquois adopted incising and smooth bodies and, in the west, undecorated rims, but generally retained grit temper. In contrast, the Monongahela Woodland continued to use cord-marked body treatment but adopted shell temper, and the Whittlesey Focus changed to incising only in a minor way. The Fort Ancient people to the south were using incised decorative techniques, appendages, and shell temper.

It now seems clear that the origin of the Iroquois culture type cannot be explained by migrations from the Southeast or the Mississippi Valley (Griffin, 1952: 364). But the stimulus for the specific changes which took place during the Early Period has not been determined. Undoubtedly it was ultimately the Mississippi cultures of this period (Griffin, 1946: 92).

Two questions remain: Did the new ideas reach and spread throughout the Iroquois area by diffusion or local movements of people, and what was the immediate source or sources of the new ideas?

Present Conclusions and Future Problems

In earlier chapters, the data on pottery vessels, pipes, projectile points, and settlement pattern have been treated comparatively for seven sites in the Niagara Frontier to select the best hypothesis stating the chronological order. Several statistical tests were employed to test their utility with small samples of data from widely scattered collections gathered under a variety of conditions. It is clear from this and other studies that quantitative differences in attributes characterize culture change through time in local Iroquois areas. It is hoped that statistical techniques will be applied to data from other Iroquois collections in New York State, the majority of which are similar to those of the Niagara Frontier in size and condition. If Iroquois culture history is to be written, much of it must be drawn painstakingly from intensive studies of collections which leave much to be desired. More refined techniques of excavation and analysis must be developed.

The chronological framework for the Niagara Frontier Region appears to be on a firm footing. The differences in the attributes and attribute combinations of pottery, pipes, projectile points, and settlement pattern support the same arrangement for the sites in this order: Oakfield, Kienuka, Shelby, Buffam Street, Eaton, Goodyear, and Green Lake. Under the assumptions made at the beginning of the study these differences are the result of temporal differences and the arrangement is the chronological one from early to late.

The concepts of Transitional Iroquois culture type and Iroquois culture type were employed to classify the culture of the seven sites. These culture types belong to the Early, and the Intermediate and Historic Periods, respectively, all subdivisions of the Late Woodland Period. These terms must be defined in the future by analysis of all possible aspects of the culture at each Iroquois site. These definitions and the understanding of the processes which led to the origin of the Iroquois remain as two of the major problems of Iroquois archaeology.

The origin or origins of the Iroquois culture type occurred during the Early Period and they must be viewed as part of a pattern of changes which were taking place in the Northeast in Late Woodland times. But the problem of origins must be worked out in local areas like that of the Niagara Frontier, where the Transitional culture type and possible antecedents are present. After a century of field work on Iroquois sites, the archaeological problems are still many times more numerous than the solutions. As these problems are solved, the results must be collated with problems of physical type and language in order to gain further understanding of Iroquois prehistory.

APPENDIX A

A COMPARISON OF THE NUMBER OF VESSELS AND RIM SHERDS

Table XI shows the comparison between the number of vessels represented by rim sherds and the number of rim sherds for each site. This comparison is expressed in Column 4, which is the ratio of the number of rims exceeding the number of vessels (Column 3 minus Column 2) to the number of rims. This is the excess of rim sherds over vessels represented by rims expressed as a percentage of the total number of rim sherds. A high percentage indicates that each vessel is represented by many rim sherds, a low percentage that each vessel is represented by comparatively few rim sherds.

TABLE XI

COMPARISON OF THE NUMBER OF VESSELS AND RIM SHERDS

1	2	3	4	5	6
Site	Number of Vessels	Number of Rims	Percentage Difference	D^2/E	D^2/E
Green Lake.	282	443	36	1.77	1.28
Goodyear	420	480	12	4.46	3.24
Eaton.	93	97	4	2.12	1.54
Buffam Street . . .	133	148	10	1.83	1.33
Shelby	232	306	24	.14	.10
Kienuka	131	209	37	1.03	.74
Oakfield	129*	270*	52*	9.04	6.58
Total	1420	1953		35.20	

*The number of rims and the difference is somewhat higher than this due to one restored vessel for which no rim sherds were included since the number could not be ascertained.

Columns 4 and 5 show the contribution of each site to the total contingency *chi square* (Spaulding, 1953: 311-12). The contingency *chi square* allows a statement of the probability that the difference between the number of rim sherds and the number of vessels for the group might occur through sampling error. The probability of obtaining a *chi square* by chance which exceeds 35.20 for 6 degrees of freedom is less than one out of one thousand. The chances of the rim sherds representing a random sample of the vessels is less than .001.

A separate consideration is whether the difference in frequency between the rim sherds and the vessels, granted that it is probably not the result of sampling error, is great enough to invalidate seriations based on an arrangement of sites by frequencies of rim sherds. Judging from some of the slight differences in percentage for certain attributes between such sites as Eaton, Buffam Street, and Goodyear, it seems likely that comparisons based on frequencies of rim sherds might result in a different arrangement.

APPENDIX B

HAND-SORTED PUNCH CARD FORM FOR POTTERY VESSELS*

Card Columns	Information
1-5	Code for identifying each site.
6-9	Provenience — midden, surface, burial, or other. Specific details of "other" recorded by hand.
10-19	Number of rim sherds representing vessel. Capacity, 1-19 sherds.
20	Kind of tempering material.
21	Kind of surface treatment of rim, neck, and body.
22-28	Lip decoration. (*a*) Incising transversely across lip. (*b*) Shallow notching across lip. (*c*) Deep notching across lip. (*d*) Circular punctations on lip. (*e*) Oval punctations on lip. (*f*) Notch on inner edge of lip. (*g*) Other lip decoration.
29-31	Lip profile. (*a*) Horizontal. (*b*) Insloping. (*c*) Outsloping.
32	Presence or absence of collar.
33-39	Width of collar. (*a*) Under 1/4″. (*b*) 1/4″ - 1/2″. (*c*) 1/2″ - 3/4″. (*d*) 3/4″ - 1″. (*e*) 1″ - 1-1/4″. (*f*) 1-1/4″ - 1-1/2″. (*g*) Over 1-1/2″ (exact width recorded).
40-50	Rim profiles. Twenty-nine different profiles coded from 1-29.
51	Vessel form, including presence of castellations and size of vessel.
52-56	Nonincised decoration above dominant motif. (*a*) Circular punctation. (*b*) Oval punctation. (*c*) Gash. (*d*) V-shaped notch in exterior edge of lip. (*e*) Other.

HAND-SORTED PUNCH CARD FORM FOR POTTERY VESSELS*

Card Columns	Information
57-63	Nonincised decoration below the dominant motif. (*a*) Circular punctation on collar. (*b*) Oval punctation on collar. (*c*) Circular punctation at junction of collar and neck. (*d*) Oval punctation at junction of collar and neck. (*e*) Circular punctation immediately below collar. (*f*) Oval punctation immediately below collar. (*g*) Other.
64	Technique of dominant motif, incised, interrupted linear, cord-wrapped stick, etc.
65	Neck decoration present or absent.
66	Atypical motifs.
67-76	Typical motifs. Eighteen motifs coded 1-18.

*Each card represents one vessel. The card is $7\frac{1}{2}$ by $3\frac{1}{4}$ inches.

APPENDIX C

COLLECTIONS AND SAMPLE SIZES USED IN THE STUDY

Oakfield Site	
Pottery Vessels	
L. L. Pechuman Collection, Lockport, New York	98
Benedict Collection, Niagara County Historical Society	8
Rochester Museum of Arts and Sciences	11
New York State Museum	12
	129
Projectile Points	
L. L. Pechuman Collection, Lockport, New York	20
New York State Museum	22
Pipes or Pipe Fragments	
L. L. Pechuman Collection, Lockport, New York	12
Kienuka	
Pottery Vessels	
R. E. McCarthy Collection, Lockport, New York	131
Projectile Points	
R. E. McCarthy Collection, Lockport, New York	34
Pipes or Pipe Fragments	
R. E. McCarthy Collection, Lockport, New York	4
Shelby	
Pottery Vessels	
Castle Collection, Buffalo Historical Society	2
Mike Hernberg Collection, Lockport, New York	4
R. E. McCarthy Collection, Lockport, New York	71
Don Owen Collection, Lockport, New York	150
Rochester Museum of Arts and Sciences	5
	232
Projectile Points	28
Pipes or Pipe Fragments	19
Buffam Street	
Pottery Vessels	
Benedict Collection, Niagara County Historical Society	39
Buffalo Museum of Science	13
Robertson Collection, Buffalo, New York	66
Museum of Anthropology, University of Michigan	15
	133

Projectile Points	72
Pipes or Pipe Fragments	14

Eaton Site

Pottery Vessels	
Benedict Collection, Niagara County Historical Society	66
New York State Museum	17
Buffalo Historical Society	4
Buffalo Museum of Science	6
	93
Projectile Points	87
Pipes or Pipe Fragments	24

Goodyear Site

Pottery Vessels	
In writer's possession	420
Projectile Points	96
Pipes or Pipe Fragments	
In writer's possession	11
Reed Collection, Buffalo Museum of Science	6
Charles Simmons Collection, East Elma, New York	4

Green Lake Site

Pottery Vessels	
Rochester Museum of Arts and Sciences	282
Projectile Points	
Rochester Museum of Arts and Sciences	43
Pipes	
Rochester Museum of Arts and Sciences	16
Reed Collection, Buffalo Museum of Science	5

BIBLIOGRAPHY

Beauchamp, William M.

1892. The Iroquois Trail or Footprints of the Six Nations. Fayetteville.

1900. Aboriginal Occupations of New York. Bull. N. Y. State Mus., Vol. 7, No. 32. Albany.

Benedict, A. L.

n.d. Unpublished Notes. Buffalo Museum of Science. Buffalo.

Brainerd, George W.

1951. The Place of Chronological Ordering in Archaeological Analysis. Amer. Antiq., 16, No. 4: 301-13. Salt Lake City.

Brebner, John Bartlet

1955. The Explorers of North America. Reprinted, 1955. Garden City.

Carpenter, E. S., K. R. Pfirman, and H. L. Schoff

1949. The 28th. Street Site. Pa. Archaeologist, XIX, Nos. 1-2: 3-16. Milton.

Champlain, Samuel de

1922. The Works of Samuel de Champlain, H. P. Biggar, ed. 6 Vols. Toronto.

Cline, Marlin G.

1955. Soils and Soil Associations. Cornell Extension Bull., No. 930. Ithaca.

Coyne, James H.

1895. The Country of the Neutrals. St. Thomas.

1903. Exploration of the Great Lakes. 1669-70. Toronto.

Crane, H. R. and James B. Griffin

1959. University of Michigan Radiocarbon Dates IV. Amer. Journ. Sci. Radiocarbon Suppl., 1: 173-98.

Crouse, Nellis M.

1924. Contributions of the Canadian Jesuits to the Geographical Knowledge of New France, 1632-1675. Ithaca.

Cushing, Frank H.

1875. Antiquities of Orleans County, New York. Ann. Rept. Board of Regents Smithsonian Instit., for the years 1874, pp. 375-77. Washington.

Cusick, David

1825. Sketches of Ancient History of the Six Nations. Tuscarora Village.

Delanglez, Jean, S.J.

1938. Some LaSalle Journeys. Instit. Jesuit Hist. Publ., Chicago.

1941. Hennepin's Description of Louisiana - A Critical Essay. *Ibid.*

1943a Franquelin, Mapmaker. Mid-Amer., 25, No. 1: 29-74. Chicago.

1943b The Sources of the Delisle Map of America, 1703. *Ibid.*, No. 4: 275-98.
1948. The Life and Voyages of Louis Joliet. Instit. Jesuit Hist. Publ. Chicago.

Edwards, Allen L.
1946. Statistical Analysis for Students in Psychology and Education. New York.

Emerson, J. Norman
n.d. The Archaeology of the Ontario Iroquois. Ph.D. Dissertation, University of Chicago, 1954.
1956. Understanding Iroquois Pottery in Ontario. Ontario Archaeolog. Soc. Toronto.
1959. A Rejoinder Upon the MacNeish-Emerson Theory. Pa. Archaeologist, 29, No. 2: 98-107. Gettysburg.

Fenneman, Nevin M.
1938. Physiography of the Eastern United States. New York.

Fenton, William N.
1940. Problems Arising from the Historic Northeastern Positions of the Iroquois. *In:* Essays in Historical Anthropology of North America. Smithsonian Misc. Colls., 100: 159-252. Washington, D. C.

Fisher, R. A.
1941. Statistical Methods for Research Workers. 8th ed. Edinburgh.

Galinée
1917. Exploration of the Great Lakes, 1669-1670 by Dollier de Casson and de Brebant de Galinée. J. H. Coyne, trans. and ed. Ontario Hist. Soc. Papers and Records, Vol. IV, Pt. 1. Toronto.

Gendron
1868. Quelque Particularitez du pays des Hurons en la Nouvelle France. Remarquees par le Sieur Gendron. Albany.

Griffin, James B.
1943. The Fort Ancient Aspect: Its Cultural and Chronological Position in Mississippi Valley Archaeology. Ann Arbor: The University of Michigan Press.
1944. The Iroquois in American Prehistory. Papers Mich. Acad. Sci., Arts, Lett., 29: 357-74. Ann Arbor.
1946. Cultural Change and Continuity in Eastern United States Archaeology. *In:* Man in Northeastern North America, Frederick Johnson, ed. Papers Peabody Found. for Archaeol., pp. 37-95. Andover.

Griffin, James B. (ed.)
1952. Archeology of the Eastern United States. Chicago: University of Chicago Press.

Guthe, Alfred K.
1955. The Hummel Site (Can. 23-3). Mus. Service, Bull. Rochester Mus. Arts Sci., Jan., 1955. Rochester.
1958. The Late Prehistoric Occupation in Southwestern New York: an Interpretive Analysis. Researches and Trans. N.Y. State Archeolog. Assn., 14, No. 1. Albany.

Hanna, Charles A.
1911. The Wilderness Trail. 2 Vols. New York.

Harris, William R.
1896. A Forgotten People: The Flint Workers. Publ. Buffalo Hist. Soc., Vol. 4. Buffalo.

Hodge, Frederick Webb
1912. Handbook of American Indians North of Mexico. Bur. Amer. Ethnol. Bull. 30, Pt. 2. Washington.

Houghton, Frederick
1899. On the Occurrence on Iroquoian Village Sites of Stone Scrapers and Perforators. Circular No. 1, Local Archaeol., Buffalo Soc. Nat. Sci. Buffalo.
1909. Indian Village, Camp and Burial Sites on the Niagara Frontier. Bull. Buffalo Soc. Nat. Sci., 9, No. 3. Buffalo.
1912. Report on Ossuary at Orangeport. *Ibid.*, 10: 471-76.
1920. History of the Buffalo Creek Reservation. Publ. Buffalo Hist. Soc., 24: 3-184. Buffalo.
1922. The Archeology of the Genesee Country. Researches and Trans. N.Y. State Archeolog. Assn., 3, No. 2. Rochester.
n.d. Unpublished Notes. Buffalo Museum of Science. Buffalo.

Hunt, George T.
1940. The Wars of the Iroquois: A Study in Intertribal Trade Relations. University of Wisconsin Press. Madison.

Johnson, Elias
1881. Legends, Traditions, and Laws of the Iroquois, or Six Nations, and History of the Tuscarora Indians. Lockport.

Jones, Arthur Edward, S.J.
1909. "8endake Ehen" or Old Huronia. Fifth Rept. Bur. Archives for the Province of Ontario. Toronto.

Jury, Wilfred
1941. Clearville Prehistoric Village Site. Bull. No. 2, Mus. Indian Archaeol., Univ. Western Ontario. London, Ontario.

Karpinski, Louis C.
1931. Map Bibliography of Michigan and the Great Lakes Region. Mich. State Hist. Soc. Lansing.

Kidd, Kenneth E.
1949. Orr Lake Pottery. Trans. Royal Canadian Instit., pp. 165-85. Toronto.

Kroeber, A. L.
1939. Cultural and Natural Areas of Native North America. Berkeley.

Lee, Thomas E.
1952. A Preliminary Report on an Archaeological Survey of Southwestern Ontario for 1950. Bull. No. 126. Ann. Rept. Nat. Mus. Canada, 1950-51, pp. 64-75. Ottawa.
1959. An Archaeological Survey of Southwestern Ontario and Manitoulin Island. Pa. Archaeologist, 39, No. 2: 80-92. Gettysburg.

MacNeish, Richard S.
1952. Iroquois Pottery Types — A Technique for the Study of Iroquois Prehistory. Nat. Mus. Canada Bull. No. 124. Ottawa.

Mayer-Oakes, William J.
1955. Prehistory of the Upper Ohio Valley; an Introductory Archeological Study (Anthropolog. Ser., No. 2). Ann. Carnegie Mus. Pittsburgh.

Morgan, Lewis H.
1851. League of the Ho-de-no-sau-nee, or Iroquois. Rochester.

Murray, Louise Welles (ed.)
1931. Selected Manuscripts of General John S. Clark. Wilkes-Barre.

Parker, Arthur C.
1907. An Erie Indian Village and Burial Site at Ripley, Chautauqua County, New York. N.Y. State Mus. Bull., No. 117, pp. 459-547. Albany.
1922. The Archaeological History of New York State. *Ibid.*, Nos. 235-36 (Pt. 1); Nos. 237-38 (Pt. 2).

Pearson, C. S. and others
1947. Soil Survey, Niagara County, New York. Ser. 1937, No. 20, United States Department of Agriculture. Washington.

Pechuman, L. L.
1958. Another Radiocarbon Date for New York State: The Oakfield Site, Genesee County. N. Y. State Archeolog. Assn. Bull. No. 14, Nov., 2958, pp. 2-4.

Phillips, Philip and Gordon R. Willey
1953. Method and Theory in American Archeology: An Operational Basis for Culture – Historical Integration. Amer. Anthropologist, 55, No. 5, Pt. 1: 615-33. Menasha.

Rider, Paul R.
1939. An Introduction to Modern Statistical Methods. New York.

Ridley, Frank
1952. The Huron and Lalonde Occupations of Ontario. Amer. Antiquity, 17, No. 3: 197-210. Salt Lake City.
1958. The Boys and Barrie Sites. Ontario Archaeolog. Soc. Publ., No. 4. Toronto.

Ritchie, William A.
1944. The Pre-Iroquoian Occupations of New York State. Rochester Mus. Memoir No. 1. Rochester.
1951. A Current Synthesis of New York Prehistory. Amer. Antiquity, 17, No. 2: 130-36. Salt Lake City.
1952. The Chance Horizon – an Early Stage of Mohawk Iroquois Cultural Development. N.Y. State Mus. Circular 29. Albany.
1954. Dutch Hollow, an Early Historic Period Seneca Site in Livingston County, New York. Researches and Trans. N.Y. State Archeolog. Assn., 13, No. 1. Albany.

Ritchie, William A., and Richard S. MacNeish
1949. The Pre-Iroquoian Pottery of New York State. Amer. Antiq., 15, No. 2: 97-124. Salt Lake City.

Robertson, Imogene C.
1952. Once an Indian Village in Buffalo. Hobbies – Mag. Buffalo Mus. Sci., 33, No. 2. Buffalo.

Robinson, W. S.
1951. A Method for Chronologically Ordering Archaeological Deposits. Amer. Antiq., 16, No. 4: 293-301. Salt Lake City.

Rouse, Irving
1955. On the Correlation of Phases of Culture. Amer. Anthropologist, 57, No. 4: 713-21. Menasha.

Sagard-Theodat, Gabriel
1866. Historie du Canada et voyages que les Freres mineurs recollects y ont faicts pour la conversion des infideles depuis l'an 1615. 4 Vols. Paris.

Sanson, N.
1658. Cartes Generales de toutes les Parties Du Monde. Paris.

Schoolcraft, H. R.
1847. Notes on the Iroquois. Albany.

Severance, Frank H.
1917. An Old Frontier of France: the Niagara Region and Adjacent Lakes under French Control. New York.

Shetrone, Henry C.
1919. The Indian in Ohio. Ohio Archaeolog. and Hist. Publ., 27: 273-510. Columbus.

Silver, Dilworth M.
1923. The Location of the Nations of Indians Called the Wenroes or Wenrohronons and the Eries. Privately printed.

Snyderman, George S.
1948. Behind the Tree of Peace. Pa. Archaeologist, 18, Nos. 3-4: 2-93. Milton.

Spaulding, Albert C.
1953. Statistical Techniques for the Discovery of Artifact Types. Amer. Antiq., 13, No. 4: 305-13. Salt Lake City.
1956. The Arzberger Site, Hughes County, South Dakota. Occ. Contrib. Mus. Anthropol. Univ. Mich., No. 16. Ann Arbor.

Squier, E. G.
1851. Antiquities of the State of New York. Buffalo.

Swanton, John R.
1952. The Indian Tribes of North America. Bur. Amer. Ethnol. Bull. 145. Washington.

Taylor, Arthur E. and others
1929. Soil Survey of Erie County, New York. Ser. 1929, No. 14, Bureau of Chemistry and Soils. Washington.

Thomas, Cyrus
1891. Report on the Mound Explorations of the Bureau of Ethnology. 12th. Ann. Rept. Bur. Ethnol., 1890-91. Washington.

Thwaites, Reuben G. (ed.)
1896-1901. The Jesuit Relations and Allied Documents. 73 Vols. Cleveland.

Turner, Orasmus
1849. Pioneer History of the Holland Purchase of Western New York. Buffalo.

Wallace, Paul A. W.
1953. Indian Highways of Pennsylvania. Pa. Archaeologist, 23, Nos. 3-4: 111-22. Milton.

White, Marian E.
1958. Dating the Niagara Frontier Iroquois Sequence. N. Y. State Archeolog. Assn. Bull. No. 14, Nov., 1958, pp. 4-9.
1959. Recent Work at Oakfield, A Transitional Iroquois Site. Eastern States Archeolog. Fed. Bull. No. 18, Oct., 1959. p. 12.

Winsor, Justin (ed.)
1884. Narrative and Critical History of America. Vol. IV. Cambridge.

Wintemberg, W. J.
1928. Uren Prehistoric Village Site, Oxford County, Ontario. Nat. Mus. Canada Bull., No. 51. Ottawa.
1939. Lawson Prehistoric Village Site, Middlesex County, Ontario. *Ibid.*, No. 94. Ottawa.
1948. The Middleport Prehistoric Village Site. *Ibid.*, No. 109. Ottawa.

Wissler, Clark
1938. The American Indian. 3d. ed. New York.

Witthoft, John
1951. Iroquois Archaeology at the Mid-Century. Proc. Amer. Philosoph. Soc., 95, No. 3: 311-21.

Witthoft, John, Harry Schoff, and Charles F Wray
1953. Micmac Pipes, Vase-Shaped Pipes, and Calumets. Pa. Archaeologist, 23, Nos. 3-4: 89-107. Milton

Wray, Charles Foster
1948. Varieties and Sources of Flint Found in New York State. *Ibid.*, 18, Nos. 1-2: 25-45. Milton.
1956. Seneca Tobacco Pipes. N. Y. State Archeolog. Assn. Bull., No. 6, March, 1956, pp. 15-16.

Wray, Charles F. and Harry L. Schoff
1953. A Preliminary Report on The Seneca Sequence In Western New York – 1550-1687. Pa. Archaeologist, 23, No. 2: 53-63. Milton.

Wright, Gordon K.
1950. The Long Point Site. *Ibid.*, 20, Nos. 3-4: 1-12.

Yates, J. V. N and J. W. Moulton
1824. History of the State of New York, including its Aboriginal and Colonial Annals. New York.

Zenkert, Charles A.
1934. The Flora of the Niagara Frontier Region. Bull. Buffalo Soc. Nat. Sci., Vol. 16, Buffalo.

PLATE I

EXAMPLES OF TECHNIQUES OF POTTERY RIM DECORATION

Fig. 1. Sherd decorated by a cord-wrapped stick. Oakfield Site, Pechuman Collection. Width, $1\frac{1}{4}$ in.

Fig. 2. Section of vessel decorated by the interrupted linear technique. Oakfield Site, Pechuman Collection. Width, $9\frac{3}{4}$ in.

Fig. 3. Sherds decorated by the interrupted linear technique. Kienuka Site, McCarthy Collection. Width, 4 in.

Fig. 4. Sherd decorated by punctations. Kienuka Site, McCarthy Collection. Width, $4\frac{1}{2}$ in.

Fig. 5. Sherds decorated by punctations. Oakfield Site, Pechuman Collection. Width, 5 in.

Fig. 6. Undecorated pottery rim. Goodyear Site. Width, $1\frac{1}{2}$ in.

Fig. 7. Incised pottery rim. Green Lake Site, Rochester Museum Collection. Width, $3\frac{1}{4}$ in.

Fig. 8. Rims decorated by "Fingernail" technique. Oakfield Site, Pechuman Collection. Width, 3 in.

PLATE I

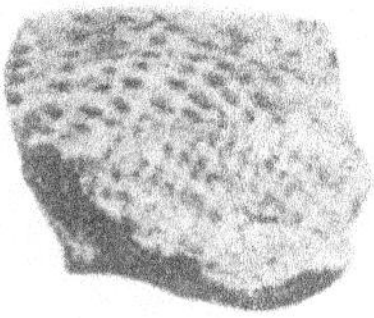

1.

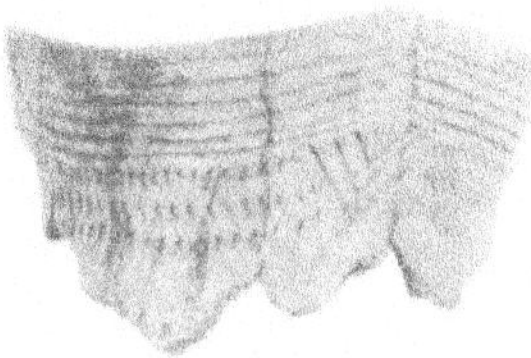

2.

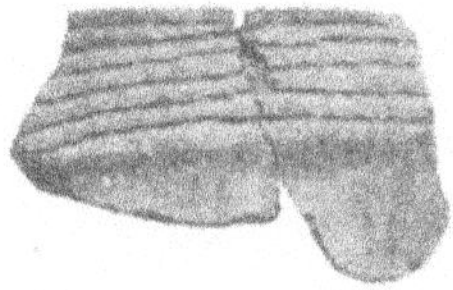

3.

4.

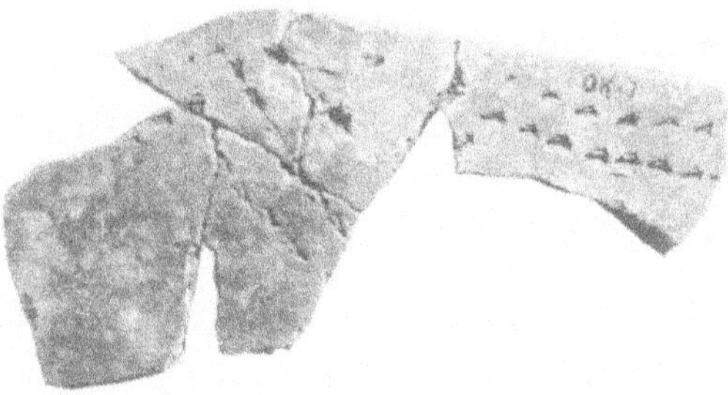

5.

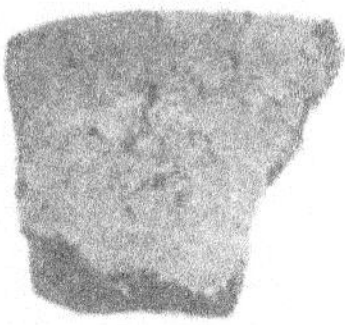

6.

7.

8.

PLATE II

SOME TYPICAL POTTERY RIM MOTIFS OF DECORATION

Fig. 1. Sherds decorated with Motif 1. Green Lake Site, Rochester Museum Collection. Width, $3\frac{3}{4}$ in.

Fig. 2. Sherd decorated with Motif 2. Buffam Street Site, Robertson Collection. Width, $2\frac{3}{4}$ in.

Fig. 3. Sherd decorated with Motif 3. Green Lake Site, Rochester Museum Collection. Width, $2\frac{1}{4}$ in.

Fig. 4. Sherd decorated with Motif 6a. Goodyear Site. Width, $1\frac{1}{2}$ in.

Fig. 5. Sherd decorated with Motif 6c. Buffam Street Site, Robertson Collection. Width, 3 in.

Fig. 6. Undecorated sherd. Goodyear Site. Width, 2 in.

Fig. 7. Section of vessel decorated to the left of the castellation with Motif 9 and to the right with Motif 1. Green Lake Site, Rochester Museum Collection. Width, 8 in.

PLATE II

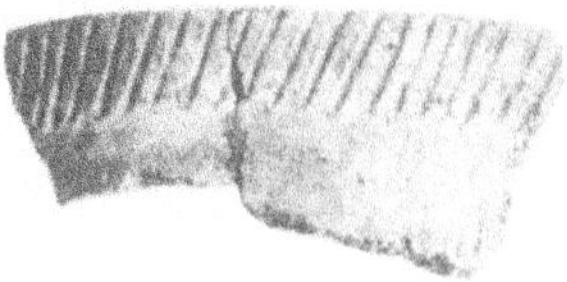

1.

2.

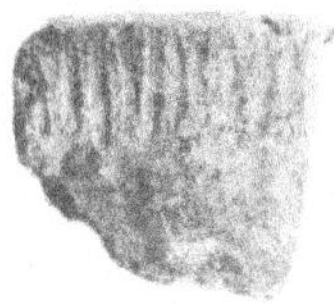

3.

4.

5.

6.

7.

PLATE III

NECK, SHOULDER, AND ADDITIONAL RIM DECORATION

Fig. 1. Sherd showing neck decoration which is a repetition of the motif of the rim decoration. Kienuka Site, McCarthy Collection. Width, $3\frac{1}{2}$ in.

Fig. 2. Sherd showing sharp shoulder and complex shoulder decoration. Green Lake Site, Rochester Museum Collection. Width, 4 in.

Fig. 3. Section of vessel showing neck decoration with a motif which is different from that of the rim. Green Lake Site, Rochester Museum Collection. Width, $7\frac{1}{4}$ in.

Fig. 4. Rim sherd decorated with punctations. Green Lake Site, Rochester Museum Collection. Width, 2 in.

Fig. 5. Sherd showing punctations above and below the rim decoration. Buffam Street Site, Robertson Collection. Width, 2 in.

Fig. 6. Sherd showing punctations at the joining of the collar and neck. Green Lake Site, Rochester Museum Collection. Width, $1\frac{1}{2}$ in.

PLATE III

1.

2.

3.

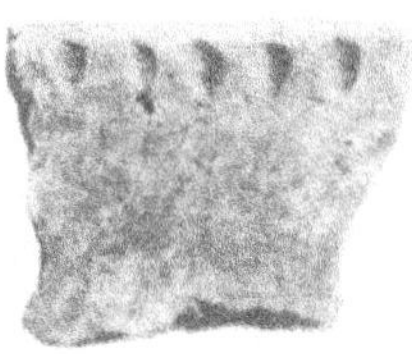

4.

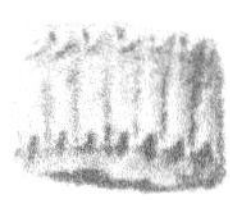

5.

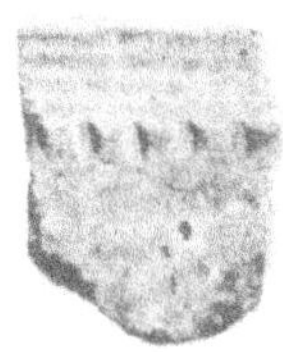

6.

PLATE IV

CASTELLATIONS ON POTTERY VESSELS

Fig. 1. Pointed castellation with oval punctations on a raised clay strip beneath the castellation. Shelby Site, Owen Collection. Width of decorated area, $2\frac{3}{4}$ in.

Fig. 2. Pointed castellation. Oakfield Site, Pechuman Collection. Width of vessel section, 10 in.

Fig. 3. Bifurcated castellation. Kienuka Site, McCarthy Collection. Width, 5 in.

Fig. 4. Squared castellation notched in two places. Green Lake Site, Rochester Museum Collection. Width, $2\frac{1}{2}$ in.

Fig. 5. Squared castellation. Green Lake Site, Rochester Museum Collection. Width, $1\frac{1}{4}$ in.

Fig. 6. Rounded castellation. Green Lake Site, Rochester Museum Collection. Width, $6\frac{1}{2}$ in.

PLATE IV

PLATE V

CLASSES OF PIPES

Fig. 1. Acorn ring bowl. Green Lake Site, Rochester Museum Collection. Length, $3\frac{1}{4}$ in.

Fig. 2. Decorated rimless trumpet. Green Lake Site, Rochester Museum Collection. Length, $5\frac{1}{4}$ in.

Fig. 3. Decorated rimmed trumpet. Buffam Street Site, Robertson Collection. Diameter of rim, $1\frac{1}{2}$ in.

Fig. 4. "Huron pipe" or square bowl. Buffam Street Site, Robertson Collection. Height, $2\frac{1}{2}$ in.

Fig. 5. Undecorated other form. Buffam Street Site, Robertson Collection. Height, $1\frac{1}{2}$ in.

Fig. 6. Human face effigy. Buffam Street Site, from a photograph in the Robertson Collection. Size unknown.

PLATE V

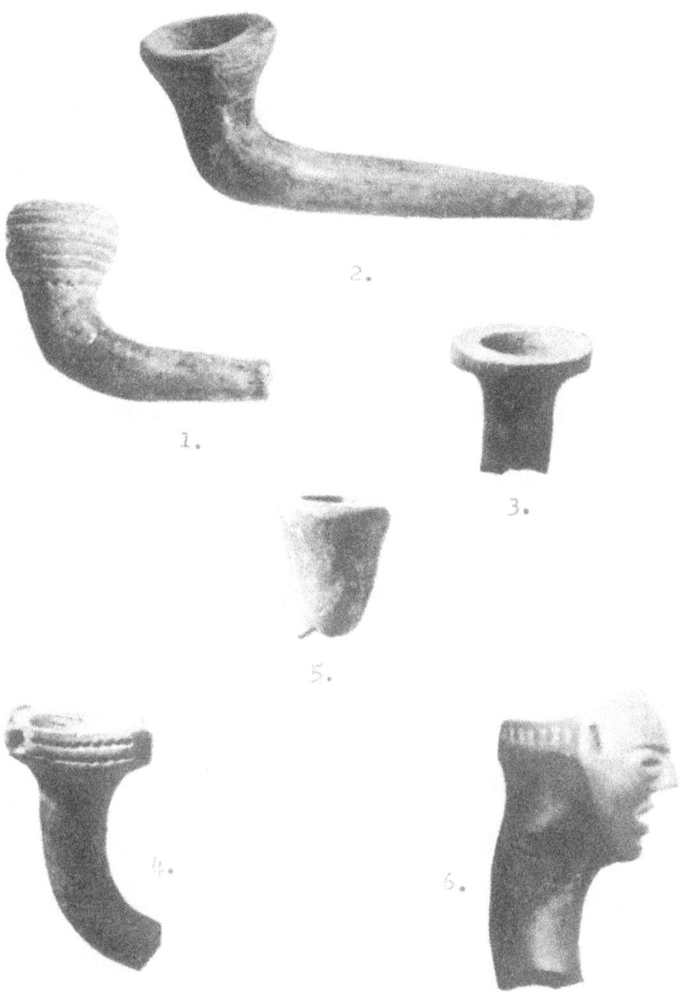

www.ingramcontent.com/pod-product-compliance
Lightning Source LLC
LaVergne TN
LVHW050021250826
846302LV00008B/54
9781949098297